Frommer's

P9-DMM-114

Banff & the Canadian Rockies
day ʙʏ day®

3rd Edition

by Christie Pashbie

Contents

Published by:

Frommer Media LLC

Copyright © 2017 FrommerMedia LLC, New York, NY. All rights reserved.
No part of this publication may be reproduced, stored in a retrieval system or transmitted in any form or by any means, electronic, mechanical,
photocopying, recording, scanning or otherwise, except as permitted
under Sections 107 or 108 of the 1976 United States Copyright Act, without the prior written permission of the Publisher. Requests to the Publisher
for permission should be addressed to Support@FrommerMedia.com.

Frommer's is a trademark or registered trademark of Arthur Frommer.

ISBN: 978-1-628-87288-0 (paper); 978-1-628-87289-7 (ebk)

Editorial Director: Pauline Frommer
Editor: Gael Cooper
Production Editor: Donna Wright
Photo Editor: Helen Stallion
Cartographer: Roberta Stockwell
Indexer: Maro Riofrancos

Front cover photos, left to right: Panithi Utamachant/Shutterstock.com,
Galyna Andrushko/Shutterstock.com, Chris Kolaczan/Shutterstock.com

Back cover photo: Jeff Whyte/Shutterstock.com

For information on our other products and services, please go to
Frommers.com.

Frommer's also publishes its books in a variety of electronic formats.
Some content that appears in print may not be available in electronic
formats.

5   4   3   2

About This Guide

Organizing your time. That's what this guide is all about.

Other guides give you long lists of things to see and do and then expect you to fit the pieces together. The Day by Day guides are different. These guides tell you the best of everything, and then they show you how to see it *in the smartest, most time-efficient way*. Our authors have designed detailed itineraries organized by time, neighborhood, or special interest. And each tour comes with a bulleted map that takes you from stop to stop.

Hoping to hike to a lookout above a glacier, ride horseback to a high alpine lake, or give rock-climbing a try? Planning to spend a few days exploring the fresh powder snow on some of the world's finest ski slopes, take a horse-drawn carriage ride under the winter stars, or mush with dog sleds across a frozen meadow? Whatever your interest or schedule, the Day by Day guides give you the smartest routes to follow. Not only do we take you to the top attractions, hotels, and restaurants, but we also help you access those special moments that locals get to experience—those "finds" that turn tourists into travelers.

The Day by Days are also your top choice if you're looking for one complete guide for all your travel needs. The best hotels and restaurants for every budget, the greatest shopping values, the wildest nightlife—it's all here.

Why should you trust our judgment? Because our authors personally visit each place they write about. They're an independent lot who say what they think and would never include places they wouldn't recommend to their best friends. They're also open to suggestions from readers. If you'd like to contact them, please send your comments our way at feedback@frommers.com, and we'll pass them on.

Enjoy your Day by Day guide—the most helpful travel companion you can buy. And have the trip of a lifetime.

About the Author

Christie Pashby is a writer, editor, and translator based in the Canadian Rockies and in Patagonia, Argentina. She has a BA from McGill University and a Bachelor of Journalism from the University of King's College. Christie has been writing guidebooks for Frommer's since 2001, covering Argentina, Chile, and Western Canada. She also runs a boutique travel company, works part-time at the Banff Mountain Film Festival, is working on a novel of historical fiction and is the mother to a preschooler who loves to hike, ski, and bike as much as her parents.

An Additional Note

Please be advised that travel information is subject to change at any time—and this is especially true of prices. We therefore suggest that you write or call ahead for confirmation when making your travel plans. The authors, editors, and publisher cannot be held responsible for the experiences of readers while traveling. Your safety is important to us, however, so we encourage you to stay alert and be aware of your surroundings.

Star Ratings, Icons & Abbreviations

Every hotel, restaurant, and attraction listing in this guide has been ranked for quality, value, service, amenities, and special features using a **star-rating system.** Hotels, restaurants, attractions, shopping, and nightlife are rated on a scale of zero stars (recommended) to three stars (exceptional). In addition to the star-rating system, we also use a **kids icon** to point out the best bets for families. Within each tour, we recommend cafes, bars, or restaurants where you can take a break. Each of these stops appears in a shaded box marked with a coffee-cup-shaped bullet 🍵.

The following **abbreviations** are used for credit cards:

AE	American Express	MC	MasterCard
DC	Diners Club	V	Visa

Frommers.com

Now that you have this guidebook to help you plan a great trip, visit our website at **www.frommers.com** for additional travel information on more than 3,600 destinations. We update features regularly to give you instant access to the most current trip-planning information available. At Frommers.com, you'll find scoops on the best airfares, lodging rates, and car rental bargains. You can even book your travel online through our reliable travel booking partners. Other popular features include:

- Online updates of our most popular guidebooks
- Vacation sweepstakes and contest giveaways
- Newsletters highlighting the hottest travel trends
- Online travel message boards with featured travel discussions

A Note on Prices

In the "Take a Break" and "Best Bets" sections of this book, we have used a system of dollar signs to show a range of costs for 1 night in a hotel (the price of a double-occupancy room) or the cost of an entree at a restaurant. Use the following table to decipher the dollar signs:

Cost	Hotels	Restaurants
$	under $100	under $10
$$	$100–$200	$10–$20
$$$	$200–$300	$20–$30
$$$$	$300–$400	$30–$40
$$$$$	over $400	over $40

An Invitation to the Reader

In researching this book, we discovered many wonderful places—hotels, restaurants, shops, and more. We're sure you'll find others. Please tell us about them, so we can share the information with your fellow travelers in upcoming editions. If you were disappointed with a recommendation, we'd love to know that, too. Please write to: Support@FrommerMedia.com.

18 Favorite
Moments

18 Favorite Moments

Gasoline

Hospital/First Aid

(i) Information

Point of Interest

Skiing

1 Gazing at the peaks from the top of Sulphur Mountain

2 Skiing the Great Divide at Sunshine Village

3 Via Ferrata at Mt. Norquay

4 Exploring an ice castle on a starry winter's night

5 Catching live jazz at the Banff Centre

6 Skating on a frozen lake

7 Hiking or cross-country skiing into Skoki Lodge

8 Hiking Lake O'Hara Alpine Circuit

9 Viewing Saskatchewan Glacier from Parker Ridge

10 Sunday brunch at the Fairmont Banff Springs

11 Soaking in the Banff Upper Hot Springs on a winter evening

12 Tea at the Plain of the Six Glaciers

13 Wildflowers at Healy Pass

14 Morning coffee run

15 Catching your first wildlife sighting

16 Setting up a mountain picnic

17 Driving the astonishing Icefields Parkway

18 Canoeing on an alpine lake

Previous page: A hiker admires the scenery along the Lake O'Hara Alpine Circuit.

Banff has been drawing visitors to the Canadian Rocky Mountains for more than a century. They're drawn primarily to nature and the peace of the wilderness. It's not necessarily hip (although Banff has trendy restaurants), and it's certainly nothing new. Banff is dependable yet surprising, a place to stretch yourself physically and reward yourself mentally. The following are some of my favorite experiences in Canada's premier mountain wilderness.

Sulphur Mountain offers the easiest summit in the Canadian Rockies.

1 Gazing at the peaks from the top of Sulphur Mountain. It's the easiest summit in the Canadian Rockies. Take the 8-minute gondola ride to the top of Sulphur Mountain, then walk the elevated 1km (⅔-mile) boardwalk to Sanson Peak, a truly jaw-dropping lookout. Six mountain ranges are displayed beneath you. There's a new restaurant and impressive interpretive displays at the top. Hardcore hikers can hike up the 5.3km (3.3-mile) switchback trail, and then reward their knees by riding the gondola down. *See p 13,* **2**.

2 Skiing the Great Divide at Sunshine Village. On a perfect winter day, catch the Continental Divide chair up to the top of Lookout Mountain, crossing from Alberta into British Columbia en route. The view of Mt. Assiniboine, the "Matterhorn of the Rockies," is magnificent, and when the powder

The Via Ferrata is a protected climbing route that can accommodate climbers of varying abilities.

is fresh and the sun is shining, your ski back down will be even more thrilling. *See p 43, Day 5.*

3 Via Ferrata at Norquay. Banff now has its own amazing Via Ferrata, an assisted climbing experience that involves crossing a series of ladders, hanging bridges and out-of-this-world views, all with an expert to lead the way. If you want some adrenaline, this is the best place to find it! *See p 153.*

4 Exploring an ice castle on a starry winter's night. Late January brings the annual Ice Magic event to the frozen shores of Lake Louise. Under the dark sky and beneath the icy glaciers of Mt. Victoria, carvers from around the world craft magical creations, culminating with a frozen castle that stays on the lake as long as the lake is frozen. Rent some skates at the Fairmont Chateau Lake Louise, snuggle by the outdoor fire, and sip hot chocolate—the ingredients of a midwinter's dream come true. *See p 160.*

5 Catching live jazz at the Banff Centre. Year-round concerts at this globally renowned arts and cultural center bring in some of the sharpest musicians from around the world. During the summer, the Banff Summer Arts Festival also showcases dance, opera, film, theater, and literary journalism. An inspiring way to spend the evening! *See p 55.*

6 Skating on a frozen lake. Clear as glass on a crisp winter day, the shallow Vermillion Lakes, close to the Town of Banff, make for a magical ice rink. The crisp mountain views and glimpses of fish wintering below the ice add to the icy drama. What could be more Canadian? Just be sure to check ice thickness with Parks Canada first. In Jasper, try Pyramid Lake. *See p 41,* **1**.

7 Hiking or cross-country skiing into Skoki Lodge. This historic cabin tucked in the woods behind Lake Louise Ski Resort may be the place that defined rustic mountain charm. The 11km (6.8-mile) trail leads to a wooden cabin with private rooms, home cooking, endless trails—and no electricity or running water. It's like stepping back in time to a pure and unspoiled mountain retreat. *See p 82.*

8 Hiking the Lake O'Hara Alpine Circuit. Just the word "O'Hara" brings oohs and aahs from veteran hikers. Across the British Columbia border behind Lake Louise, in Yoho National Park, this is an exquisite hiking destination, dotted with meadows, lookouts, ridge-walks, turquoise lakes, and meticulously chiseled stone trails. There are a half-dozen superb hikes to choose from, but the Alpine Circuit highlights the best of the best. Remember to book your bus ride up to the lake well in advance. *See p 25, Day 9.*

9 Viewing the Saskatchewan Glacier from Parker Ridge. Hike for just over an hour for views even more stunning than those you can see from your car on the Icefields Parkway. The trail starts steeply, but

The crystal clear surface of Lake O'Hara sparkles in Yoho National Park.

The alpine wildflowers at Healy Pass are picture-perfect in July and August.

soon plateaus out into the subalpine zone, offering gorgeous views of the Saskatchewan Glacier and Mt. Athabasca. Don't forget to look down and around you too—you may see fossils, rosy finches, mountain goats, and maybe even a grizzly bear. For solitude and spectacular vistas, few short hikes in the world can compare. *See p 46,* **7**.

🔟 Sunday brunch at the Fairmont Banff Springs. In the stately Bow Valley Grill inside this legendary hotel, you can sample a stellar array of gourmet Canadiana, from smoked Wild Pacific salmon and free-range eggs Benedict, to roasted Alberta beef and maple brownies. Ask for a window table for views of Fairholme Range and Bow River, and bring your appetite. Reservations recommended. *See p 14,* **3**.

⓫ Soaking in the Banff Upper Hot Springs on a winter evening. If it's cold and you've been skiing all day, you're in the right town—just head to the historic bathhouse to relax in the natural hot pools (ranging from 99°–104°F/37°–40°C), open until 10pm weeknights in winter and 11pm on winter weekends. Other hot springs in the mountain parks worth visiting include Miette Hot

Springs in Jasper National Park and the Radium Hot Springs in Kootenay National Park. *See p 14,* **7**.

⓬ Tea at the Plain of the Six Glaciers. Drawing hikers since 1924, this historic tea house is a rustic cabin nestled in a gorgeous location at the back of Lake Louise. It's a 2-hour hike to get here—surely you deserve a piece of chocolate cake or banana loaf? Take your pot of tea and sit outside to marvel at the six glaciers that cling to Aberdeen, Lefroy, Victoria, and Popes Peak. *See p 146.*

⓭ Wildflowers at Healy Pass. In the high alpine zone, hardy wildflowers like moss Campion, purple Saxifrage, glacier lilies, and alpine forget-me-nots bloom into gorgeous colors from mid-July to mid-August. This pass just beside Sunshine Village ski area is one of the finest areas for these brilliant displays. Hike the 12km (7.5-mile) trail up to alpine meadows, or cheat by taking the Sunshine Meadows shuttle up most of the way. In Jasper, head to Mt. Edith Cavell. *See p 100,* **8**.

⓮ Morning coffee run. Early morning is the quietest time of the day on the otherwise-bustling main strip of Banff Avenue. Before 9am,

Canoeing on a serene alpine lake.

it's the peaceful terrain of locals. Join them for a cafe latte and some homemade granola (served with berry compote and yogurt) at the Wild Flour Bakery. As the workers head off, relish your vacation time with a stroll along the Bow River. In Jasper, do the same at the Bear's Paw Bakery. *See p 127.*

⓯ Catching your first wildlife sighting. Whether it's an elk munching on grass on a lawn or a grizzly bear crossing an avalanche path, each glimpse of a wild animal in Banff is a gift. There are no guarantees, but there's a good chance that you'll see bighorn sheep at Lake Minnewanka at dusk or dawn. Some animals, of course, require more seriousness than others. Visit the Parks Canada Visitors Centres for more information. *See p 13, ❶.*

⓰ Setting up a mountain picnic. Quieter than the Trans-Canada Highway, the Bow Valley Parkway's best picnic spot is at the Storm Mountain Lookout, just north of Castle Junction, for great views and photo-ops. Pick up supplies for a picnic at Nester's Market in Banff or at Laggan's in Lake Louise. *See p 142.*

⓱ Driving the astonishing Ice-fields Parkway. For 230km (143 miles), drive a road that feels like it's been carved inside the earth, with massive mountains clinging to the Continental Divide, ancient glaciers, and ragged peaks. At the middle are the Columbia Icefields, the liquid heart from which the waters of the nation pump. Oh, and there are mountain goats and grizzly bears too! *See p 64.*

⓲ Canoeing on an alpine lake. Emerald, Maligne, Moraine . . . their names simply invite you to grab a paddle and launch a canoe upon their sublime shores. Out alone (or with a friend) on a placid alpine lake, with your reflection blending with that of giant rocky peaks on the ripples beside you, you'll find you're living inside your own postcard from paradise. Moraine Lake is next to Lake Louise and is less visited but still easy to access, making it my top choice. *See p 63, ❾.* ●

1 Strategies for Seeing **Banff & the Canadian Rockies**

Banff & the Canadian Rockies

Previous page: Photo opportunities can arise anywhere—even on the road between sites.

The beautiful Canadian Rockies are a vast area with so much to see and do. Your time is precious and you need to plan according to the seasons, the length of your visit, and your goals and tastes. Don't try to do it all—the magic in Banff is in the quietest moments. In this chapter, I have several tips to help you make the most of your time.

The Lake Louise Visitor Centre provides maps, permits, and park information.

Rule #1: Get out of town!
While the Town of Banff holds most of the lodgings and restaurants, not to mention shops and nightlife, it's what you'll find in the rest of the park that will most astound you. Those particularly interested in solitude should head to a nearby national park—Jasper in the north, or Kootenay and Yoho to the west—or to one of the many backcountry lodges dotted throughout the park. Even day trips in a car or a short hike count towards spreading your wings here.

Rule #2: Go to the experts and visit the Parks Canada Information Centres
These should be your first stop, whether it's in the Town of Banff, at Lake Louise, or in Jasper. Pick up maps and permits and take in interpretive exhibits that will greatly enhance your experience in the Canadian Rockies. The friendly staff members have the latest trail, road, avalanche, and wildlife reports, and can answer just about any question you have.

Rule #3: Don't over-schedule
Jam-packing your days from an early-morning bird-watching trip to a late-night stargazing excursion will only leave you exhausted. The loveliest moments in Banff are those that surprise you—spotting a wolf on a quiet road, or having a leisurely picnic by the river. Give yourself time for spontaneous adventure and explorations.

Rule #4: Allow plenty of travel time
Not only are the distances great, but you'll find lots of mountains along the way that provide twists and turns—there are few straight lines in the Canadian Rockies. And along the way from A to B, there'll likely be dozens of photo opportunities and

Mountains at every turn can make for winding roads and slow driving.

maybe even some wildlife sightings. Plan to get out of the car often, and take your time while driving.

Rule #5: Come in the shoulder season

Not only will it save you money, but you'll avoid the crowds. June is considered off-season, and September (my favorite month in Banff) is great for hiking. For winter travelers, try pre-Christmas December for good deals and April for spring skiing.

Rule #6: Be prepared for weather

In the Rockies, it's common to see all four seasons in a single day, any time of the year. Even in the middle of summer, don't be surprised to see snow—bring appropriate clothing and never hit the trail without a good jacket, hat, sunscreen, and a bottle of water.

Rule #7: Try something new

Banff is a great place to do

Carefree skiing in the off-season.

something you've never done before—or something you haven't done in years. Hiking isn't just for the super-fit and horseback riding ain't only for cowboys. The campground up at Lake O'Hara may be the most accessible backcountry camping in the mountains, so give it a try. In wintertime, take a snowboard lesson or try ice skating. Vacations are for breaking free!

Rule #8: Pick one central activity each day, then plan around it

For days when you plan to head out for a hike or to hit the slopes, get prepared the evening before. Pack food, get your gear ready, and check the latest conditions. And get a good night's sleep! Be logical so that you don't have to back-track.

Rule #9: Think outside the park

Save cash by staying in a hotel just outside Banff. The Town of Canmore, just 20km (12 miles)— a 15-minute drive—east of Banff, is a lovely mountain town with an impressive list of affordable hotel options and fabulous restaurants.

Rule #10: Use this book as a reference, not a concrete plan

Don't worry; I won't be hurt if you don't follow every single tour I lay out here. Read through the options I present, pick the ones that most appeal to you, and adapt them to your personal circumstances. ●

2 The Best Full-Day Tours

Banff in Three Days

DAY 1
1. Banff Information Centre
2. Banff Gondola
3. Fairmont Banff Springs Hotel
4. Coyotes Grill
5. Tunnel Mountain
6. The Bison
7. Upper Hot Springs

DAY 2
8. Lake Louise Village
9. Laggan's Mountain Deli
10. Lake Louise
11. Fairmont Chateau Lake Louise
12. Tea at the Chateau
13. Moraine Lake
14. Bow Valley Parkway

DAY 3
15. Crowfoot Glacier
16. Peyto Lake
17. Saskatchewan Crossing
18. Columbia Icefields
19. The Glacier Adventure and Skywalk

Gasoline
Information
Point of Interest
Skiing

Previous page: Canoeing is a beautiful way to explore Banff's tranquil lakes.

L ocated at the confluence of the Spray and Bow rivers, and on the lower slopes of Tunnel and Sulphur mountains, the Town of Banff is rich in culture and history, with adventure at your doorstep.

Travel Tip

Avoid parking hassles by using the ROAM hybrid bus system, which runs down all the routes mentioned below. An unlimited day pass costs $5. For more information call ☎ 403/762-0606; www.roamtransit.com. Days 2 and 3 require your own vehicle.

Day 1

❶ ★★ Banff Information Centre. No visit to Banff should start anywhere else. Stock up on maps and free self-guided tour brochures, and get helpful advice from the knowledgeable and friendly staff of the Parks Canada, Banff/Lake Louise Tourism Bureau, and Friends of Banff desks. ⏱ *30 min. 224 Banff Ave.* ☎ *403/762-1550. Sept 6–June 19 9am–5pm; June 20–Sept 6 9am–7pm. Closed Dec 25.*

Hop on the ROAM bus 1 or drive up Banff Avenue over the Bow River Bridge. Take a left after the bridge onto Spray Avenue and a quick right up Mountain Road until you arrive at:

The Banff Gondola.

❷ ★ kids Banff Gondola. A quick 8-minute gondola ride takes you to the top of the 2,285m (7,496 ft.) Sulphur Mountain. Walk the elevated boardwalk to Sanson Peak. Bring at least a sweater! ⏱ *70 min. At the end of Mountain Rd., 2.5km (1½ miles) from Banff Ave.* ☎ *403/762-2523. www.brewster.ca. Adults $41, kids 6 and up $21. Kids under 6 free. Mid-Oct to mid-May 10am–6pm; mid-May to June 30 9am–9pm;*

The staff at the Banff Information Centre are knowledgeable and eager to help.

Nonguests can enjoy the Fairmont Banff Springs Hotel over a meal or short tour.

July 1–Sept 5 8am–10pm; Sept 6 to mid-Oct 8am–7pm.

Head back down Mountain Road, taking a right at Spray Avenue. If you are on the ROAM bus 1, you'll have to change lines on to bus 2 at the corner of Spray Avenue and Mountain Road. Continue to the right until you arrive at:

❸ ★★ Fairmont Banff Springs Hotel. You can't miss the unmistakable stone towers and green roof of this national landmark. Ostentatious and oozing with amenities, it's an expensive place to stay (see p 79), but a marvelous building and certainly a must-see on any trip to Banff. Nonguests are welcome to grab a meal, visit the spa, or take a short tour of the hotel. ⏲ *45 min. 405 Spray Ave.* ☎ *403-762-2211. www.fairmont.com/banff.*

From the Banff Springs, head back down Banff Avenue into town. Turn left on Caribou Street to:

❹ Lunch at Coyotes Grill. Few places have stood the test of time as well as this Southwest-inspired bistro in the heart of Banff. Run by devoted locals, the food is fresh and tasty. Try a corn-crusted pizza or chicken enchilada. *206 Caribou St.* ☎ *403-762-3963. www. coyotesbanff.com. $$*

Leave the streets behind, walking up Wolf Street towards the Banff Centre, keeping an eye out for the trail head for:

❺ ★★ Tunnel Mountain Hike. Work off lunch by hiking this classic Banff trail that heads right out of the heart of town. It's a 2.3km (1.4-mile) hike that takes you 300m (984 ft.) up to the summit. One of the oldest trails in the park, this is very popular with Banff locals. ⏲ *2½ hr. Trail head is at St. Julien Rd., 300m (984 ft.) uphill from the Wolf St. junction.*

Head back into town on Wolf Street, turning left on Bear Street. Half a block down, you'll find:

❻ The Bison. Hit the sunny patio here for a treat. Overlooking Bear Street and Mt. Rundle, it's got the best view of any patio in town. Upscale cheese and meat trays make great appetizers, and there's a long wine-by-the-glass menu and local beers on tap. *See p 71. 211 Bear St.* ☎ *403-762-5550. www.thebison.ca. $$.*

After a leisurely meal, hop back on the ROAM bus 1 or drive up Mountain Road towards:

❼ ★★ Upper Hot Springs. For more than a century, visitors have come to Banff to "take the waters." Evenings are the best time at these historic pools. ⏲ *60 min. At the end of Mountain Rd., 2.5km (1½ miles) from downtown Banff.* ☎ *403-762-1515. Oct 31–Dec 25 Sun–Thurs 10am–10pm, Fri–Sat 10am–11pm; Dec 25–Jan 2 10am–11pm; Jan 3 to mid-May Sun–Thurs 10am–10pm, Fri–Sat 10am–11pm; mid-May to mid-Oct 9am–11pm. Adult $7, seniors and children (3–17) $6.*

It's hard to take a bad photo of lovely Lake Louise.

Day 2

Your day begins with a delightful 45-minute drive to Lake Louise. Head straight there from Banff—you'll have time later in the afternoon to look around the Bow Valley. Your goal is to beat the crowds to the lake and to secure the best light for photographing.

❶ ★ Lake Louise Village. A small "'hamlet" just off the Trans-Canada Highway, this is a collection of hotels, restaurants, gas stations, and shops centered at the Samson Mall. Pick up a snack or grab a new fleece if the weather has soured. The Parks Canada Information Centre is just behind the shopping plaza, worth a visit for trail and wildlife updates. ⏱ *40 min. 58km (36 miles) west of Town of Banff on Trans-Canada Hwy. 1.*

❷ Laggan's Mountain Deli. This unpretentious coffee and sandwich shop is popular with hikers, bikers, skiers, and anybody on the move. It's in the middle of Samson Mall. Beat the crowds by entering the alternative door on the left side and heading for the second cashier. *101 Lake Louise Dr., in Samson Mall. ☎ 403/522-2017. $.*

Drive out of the Samson Mall parking lot onto Village Road, turning left at Lake Louise Drive and head up the hill until you reach:

❸ ★★★ Lake Louise. Perhaps the most photographed lake in Canada, this stunner draws thousands of visitors every week from every corner of the globe. At the back of the lake, Mt. Victoria and the Victoria Glacier make an imposing backdrop. Take an hour to stroll to the back of the lake. Find a quiet spot for a snack.

It's impossible to miss the massive building to your right:

❹ ★★ Fairmont Chateau Lake Louise. This landmark hotel is known as "'the diamond in the wilderness." For more than 125 years, mountaineers, artists, and lovers of the outdoors have been drawn to the sublime landscape outside of, and the grace inside of, this hotel. ⏱ *30 min. 111 Lake Louise Dr. ☎ 403/522-1818. www.fairmont.com/lake-louise.*

❺ Tea at the Chateau. If you're not a guest, you can experience the refined elegance of this famous hotel by reserving a table for afternoon tea in the Lakeview Lounge. By reservation only. *111 Lake Louise Dr. ☎ 403/522-1818. $$.*

Drive out of the parking lot and take the first right on the Moraine Lake Road, which leads you to:

❻ ★★★ Moraine Lake. Some say Louise's less-visited sister lake is even more beautiful. Wild and dramatic, Moraine Lake is surrounded by 10 spire-like peaks. There's a great interpretive trail to the Moraine Lake Rockpile. ⏱ *45 min. 13km (8 miles) south of Lake Louise on Moraine Lake Rd.*

Dramatic Moraine Lake is surrounded by peaks.

Bid farewell to the Lake Louise area, driving back down to the village. Drive over the Trans-Canada Highway, taking the next right on to:

⑦ Bow Valley Parkway 1A.

Built in 1920, the first road connecting Banff and Lake Louise still feels more like a mountain road than an expressway. Compared to the Trans-Canada Highway, the Parkway is quieter and gives you a much better chance for wildlife sightings.

The day ends returning on the Bow Valley Parkway 1A and then finally on the Trans-Canada Highway into the Town of Banff.

Day 3

One of the most beautiful drives in the entire world, a day on the Icefields is not to be missed. Continuing north on the Icefields Parkway from Lake Louise, the road steadily climbs higher and higher and the views become more and more dramatic as you make your way through three river valleys and pass beneath towering glacier-topped peaks. Get an early start, as the first stop is over an hour from Banff.

Travel Tip

Food options are next-to-nonexistent once you pass Lake Louise, so pick up a picnic there or in Banff. You must have a valid Park Pass to drive on this highway. See p 59.

① ★ Crowfoot Glacier. The

first of a long line-up of glaciers you'll see once resembled the foot of a crow (hence the name), but has shrunk significantly. There are interpretive signs posted at the roadside viewpoint. ⏱ *10 min. 32km (20 miles) from Lake Louise on Hwy. 93, the Icefields Parkway.*

Crowfoot Glacier, one of the many breathtaking sights along the Icefields Parkway.

Continue north on the Icefields Parkway to:

② ★★ Peyto Lake. There is a short interpretive trail to this beautifully turquoise gem, named for pioneer guide Bill Peyto, who was also a warden in Banff National Park. ⏱ *20 min. 42km (26 miles) from Lake Louise on Hwy. 93, the Icefields Pkwy.*

Continue north on the Icefields Parkway to:

③ Saskatchewan Crossing. This is the only place with any kind of services between Lake Louise and the Icefield Centre. Besides lovely views of the Mistaya, Howse, and North Saskatchewan river valleys, there is a warden station, gas station, snack bar, and gift shop. ⏱ *10 min. 50 km (31 miles) from Lake Louise on Hwy. 93, the Icefields Pkwy.*

Continue north on the Icefields Parkway to:

④ ★★★ Columbia Icefield. Just north of the Banff-Jasper park border, this is an area of glacial ice and snow measuring 190 sq. km (73 sq. miles) that is up to 350m (1,148 ft.) deep in places. It'll give you an idea what the northern part of North America may have looked like during the Earth's last ice age. There are six main glaciers flowing from the Columbia Icefield. Park at the Icefield Centre, the main building in the area. This is where you need to go to sign up for a tour on the Columbia Icefield's giant snocoach. ⏱ *2–3 hr. total. 125km (78 miles) from Lake Louise on Hwy. 93, the Icefield Pkwy.* ☎ *780/852-6288. May 1 to late Sept 10am–5pm. Closed late Sept to Apr 30.*

Directly across the highway is:

⑤ ★★ kids The Glacier Adventure and Skywalk. Take a giant snocoach onto the Athabasca Glacier, which drops you off in the middle of the ice where you can walk around. Then, walk out on a glass-floored platform overlooking the Sunwapta Valley. Expect to have to wait for availability in tours, especially in July and August. Come early or late for shorter wait times. Tours leave every 15 minutes or so. ⏱ *120 min. 125km (78 miles) from Lake Louise on Hwy. 93, the Icefields Pkwy.* ☎ *403/762-6735. www.brewster.ca. Kids under 5 free. Adventure adults $57, kids 6–15 $29; Skywalk adults $32, kids 6–15 $16. Apr 15–29 and Oct 3–16 10am–4pm, Apr 30–May 27 10am–5pm, May 28–Sept 4 9am–6pm, Sept 5–Oct 2 10–5pm.*

The day ends retracing your steps back to Banff on Hwy. 93 and then on the Trans-Canada Hwy. 1.

The lookout onto Peyto Lake is a short hike away from Icefields Parkway.

Best in One Week

0 10 mi	⛽ Gasoline
0 10 km	ⓘ Information
	◻ Point of Interest

To Jasper National Park

ⓘ
4

LYELL ICEFIELD

93

Park Gate

Saskatchewan Crossing

11

Siffleur Wilderness

ALBERTA

Icefields Parkway

93

FRESHFIELD ICEFIELD

BRITISH COLUMBIA

BANFF NATIONAL PARK

Red Deer River

WAPTA ICEFIELD

Kicking Horse Pass

Bow River

6e **6f**

6b

6a

ⓘ

YOHO NATIONAL PARK

Field

ⓘ

Lake Louise Village

5

3

7

6c **6d**

1

Temple Mtn.

Castle Mtn.

Cascade Mtn.

Golden

Columbia River

Castle Junction

Johnston Canyon

Park Gate

KOOTENAY NATIONAL PARK

1

1A

1

Banff

2

93

Mt. Assiniboine Provincial Park

Radium Hot Springs

Park Gate

40 Edmonton
16 ALBERTA
Jasper 93 2
BRITISH COLUMBIA
Lake Louise
Golden Banff Calgary
2
Area of map
CANADA
UNITED STATES
16

1 Town of Banff
2 Horseback riding at the Spray River
3 Lake Louise
4 Icefields Parkway
5 Hiking at Lake Louise
6 Yoho National Park
   6a Spiral Tunnels
   6b Takakkaw Falls
   6c Field
   6d Siding General Store and Café
   6e Emerald Lake
   6f Cilantro on the Lake
7 Biking at Lake Louise

Having a few extra days allows you time to explore the backcountry of Banff National Park, and visit the historically—and geographically—fascinating Yoho National Park, next door to Banff. You can blend both active adventures, like hiking and horseback riding, with traditional touring and sightseeing.

Day 1
Follows the Town of Banff tour from Day 1 above.

Day 2
Saddle up today to head into the mountains. Follow in the steps of cowboys, pack guides, and wilderness explorers near Banff. **Banff Trail Riders,** who have run trail rides in Banff for nearly 50 years, has a full-day trip that heads up the Spray River and includes a barbecue lunch (see p 154). *132 Banff Ave.* 📞 *800/661-8352 or 403/762-4551.*

Day 3
Today follows Day 2 of "Banff in 3 Days" with one difference: Drive up to Lake Louise on the Bow Valley Parkway, stopping at Johnston Canyon and Muleshoe en route (see p 59), and plan on spending the next few nights based out of Lake Louise after visiting the area.

Day 4
Today follows Day 3 of "Banff in 3 Days," taking in all the highlights of

Trail riding up the Spray River.

the spectacular Icefields Parkway, returning to Lake Louise in the evening.

Day 5
Lake Louise hiking: In a land of superlatives, there are many outstanding hiking options to choose from. The classic Lake Louise hike, the Highline Trail, connects Lake Agnes with the Plain of the Six Glaciers, two historic tea houses, massive glaciers, and a lovely, gentle downhill finish. *Tip:* Pick up lunch supplies at Laggan's in Samson Mall, and be sure to bring plenty of water! *See chapter 6 for trail descriptions.*

Day 6
Yoho National Park: "Yoho" is an expression of awe and wonder in the Cree language, and that's just what you'll experience in this park, located just over the provincial border from Banff in British Columbia. Yoho showcases the western slopes of the Rockies with dozens of spectacular waterfalls and the Kicking Horse River. It's also an interesting spot for history buffs.

Take the Trans-Canada Hwy. 1 west from Lake Louise 9.2km (5¾ miles) to the border between Alberta and British Columbia. 8.7km (5½ miles) west of the border, turn off into the roadside interpretive display at:

❶ ★ Spiral Tunnels. Steep as it is, the CPR (Canadian Pacific Railway) in the 1880s selected the Kicking Horse Pass as the easiest way over the Rockies. But it was still very, very steep, and soon enough trains were crashing down the socalled "Big Hill." The Spiral Tunnels were designed more than 100 years

A train emerging from Cathedral Mountain through the Spiral Tunnels.

through the tunnels, though not on a regular schedule).

Continue down the hill on the Trans-Canada Highway another 3.7km (2¼ miles), turning right at Yoho Valley Road for:

❷ ★★ **Takakkaw Falls.** Reach the fourth-highest waterfall in Canada by driving up the Kicking Horse River on Yoho Valley Road (not recommended for large RVs or trailers). If you love waterfalls, you've come to the right place. Hike in another hour along the Yoho Valley trail past Staircase Falls and Point Lace Falls to see Laughing Falls and then on to beautiful Twin Falls.

Drive back out to the Trans-Canada Hwy. 1, continuing 1.8km (1 mile) west to the Field turnoff.

ago to take trains through two loops dug inside Cathedral Mountain, easing the grade. View the Spiral Tunnels from the side of Trans-Canada Hwy. 1 just up the hill from Field; there are excellent interpretive signs, and if your timing's good, you'll actually catch a train going through the tunnels (on an average day, 25 to 30 trains pass

❸ ★ **Field.** With a population of only 200 souls, the tiny town of Field, BC has a gorgeous setting beside the Kicking Horse River and beneath Mt. Stephen. There are a few charming shops, including the Velvet Antler Pottery ⏱ *30 min. (on Stephen Ave. next to Siding Café,* ☎ *250/343-6456). 27km (17 miles) from Lake Louise.*

Takakkaw Falls in Yoho National Park.

Cilantro on the Lake provides stunning alpine views in summertime.

Head through tiny Field, turning right on Kicking Horse Avenue, and make a quick U-turn at Stephen Avenue to find:

4 ★ Siding General Store and Café.
A cozy deli in historic Field is a good stop any time of day: pre-hike for a breakfast sandwich or to get a "designer" sandwich to go. Or come by post-hike for a date square, brownie, and cup of tea. It's even open for dinner, with salads, pastas, and a great veggie chili. *318 Stephen Ave., at the corner of Kicking Horse Ave.* ☎ *250/343-6002. www.thesidingcafe.ca. $$.*

Back out on the Trans-Canada Highway, turn left (west) and continue 2km (1¼ miles) to the turnoff for Emerald Lake Road. Drive 8km (5 miles) until you reach:

5 ★★ Emerald Lake.
Move past the crowded parking lot and hike the lovely 5km (3.1-mile) trail around this marvelous alpine lake. With just a little bit of up and down, this wide trail that circles the pristine Emerald Lake is rich and delightful, almost easy enough to be considered a stroll. Legendary local guide Tom Wilson is credited for having "discovered" this natural marvel in 1882 as part of a

route-scouting for the Canadian Pacific Railroad. This is a great family outing or leg-stretcher; it showcases a gem of a lake, and the interpretive signs are informative.

6 ★ Cilantro on the Lake.
Open only during the summertime, this is a pretty mountain bistro at Emerald Lake Lodge offering wood-fired flatbread pizzas, gourmet burgers, and micro-brewed beer in a sublimely beautiful setting. Sit on the lovely, sunny patio overlooking Emerald Lake or inside the spectacular timber-frame lodge. *On Emerald Lake Rd., 8km (5 miles) off Trans-Canada Hwy., at a turnoff 2km (1¼ miles) south of Field.* ☎ *250/343-6321. www.crmr.com/emerald. $$*

Day 7
Your final day is for some morning adventure. Rent a mountain bike from **Wilson Mountain Sports** in Samson Mall (from $39/day; ☎ 866/929-3636 or 403/522-2178; www.wmsll.com) and ride the 9km (5.6-mile) return classic Tramline Trail. Families will prefer the gentle Bow River Loop or the Great Divide Bike Path, which is better suited to a road bike. Then give yourself plenty of time to say goodbye to the Rockies and head out.

Best in Two Weeks

DAY 1
1 Town of Banff

DAY 2
2 Horseback Riding on the Spray River

DAY 3
3 Sunshine Meadows

DAY 4
4 Kootenay National Park

DAY 5
5 Lake Louise

DAY 6
6 Hiking in Paradise Valley/ Larch Valley

DAY 7
7 Yoho National Park

DAY 8
8 Camping at Lake O'Hara

DAY 9
9 Hiking at Lake O'Hara

DAY 10
10 Icefields Parkway

DAY 11
11 Tour of Jasper Townsite and Area

DAY 12
12 Maligne Valley

DAY 13
13 Rafting the Athabasca River

DAY 14
14 Breakfast at Bear's Paw

Lucky are those with time to linger in the Canadian Rockies. After all, there are nearly 23,000 sq. km (8,880 sq. ft.) of mountain wilderness to explore, and that takes time. Blending sightseeing with active adventures, and allowing you to roam from Banff up to Jasper, this is perhaps the ultimate 2-week vacation in this inimitable setting. Just be sure to book ahead of time, particularly your night at Yoho National Park's Lake O'Hara—either the campground or the historic and peerless Lake O'Hara Lodge. For more details see p 137.

Day 1
See Day 1 from the "Banff in 3 Days" tour, p 13.

Day 2
Aim to hit the trail today on horseback. See Day 2 of "Best in 1 Week," p 19.

Day 3
★★ kids **Sunshine Meadows.**
When the snow melts at the world-famous Sunshine Village ski area, the alpine meadows blossom into a multicolored dreamland hugging the Continental Divide, great for moderate hiking amidst more than 340 species of wildflowers. The Garden Path Trail is breathtaking in late July and August. To the south you can see Mount Assiniboine, the "Matterhorn of the Rockies." Take a bus from the parking lot or right from the Town of Banff and skip the arduous uphill hike. *Tip:* Book the morning buses ahead of time, and don't forget to bring a lunch and

bear spray, drink water, and use plenty of sunscreen. *8km (5 miles) west of Banff on the Sunshine Rd.* ☎ *403/762-7889. $26 adults, $15 children 3–12. June 19–Sept 15 9am–5:30pm.*

Day 4
★★ kids **Kootenay National Park.** Less visited, and wonderfully expansive, Kootenay is an off-the-beaten-path destination that makes a great day trip from Banff. This park is particularly friendly to families, with lots of kids in strollers and some great picnic spots.

Drive the Trans-Canada Hwy. 1 west to Castle Junction and take Hwy. 93 south. Length: 132km (82 miles) each way.

Travel Tip

Driving Hwy. 93 at dusk is prime wildlife-viewing time, so keep an eye out and drive safely.

A sunny day at Sunshine Meadows.

1 ★ kids Fireweed Trail. A 20-minute loop explains why natural forest fires are healthy and good for the environment. As you continue on through Kootenay, you may be driving through a number of fire sites, so getting the low-down here will help you understand and appreciate the burned landscapes. ⏱ *15 min. 95km (59 miles) from Radium, on the Alberta–British Columbia (and Banff–Kootenay) border.*

Continue southwest of Hwy. 93.

2 ★★ Stanley Glacier. One of my favorite shorter hikes in the Rockies, this trail takes you from fire (a lightning-provoked burn from 1968) to ice (the Stanley Glacier) in just 2.5km (1.5 miles). Most of the 395m (1,296 ft.) to be climbed are at the beginning, leaving you time to amble amidst a hanging valley with awesome views. Great for families. ⏱ *3 hr. Trail head is 3.2km (2 miles) west of the Alberta–British Columbia (and Banff–Kootenay national parks) border on south side of highway.*

3 Marble Canyon. A narrow trail of limestone carved by two retreating glaciers, this is a great spot on a hot day. It's cool and shady. Kids will find this short hike intriguing, but keep a sharp eye on them because the trail can get very slippery. ⏱ *30 min. 89km (55 miles) from Radium, 7km (4⅓ miles) from*

Alberta–British Columbia (and Banff–Kootenay national parks) border on north side of highway.

4 ★ Paint Pots. Natives came together at these remote cold springs to gather ocher, an iron-based mineral that was baked, crushed, mixed with grease, and used as a paint for teepees, pictographs, and personal adornment. There's an excellent wheelchair and stroller-friendly 30-minute interpretive trail. ⏱ *40 min. 85km (53 miles) from Radium, 10km (6¼ miles) from Alberta–British Columbia (and Banff–Kootenay national parks) border on north side of highway.*

5 ★★ Radium Hot Springs Pool. Nestled in a canyon rich with oxide, these "sacred mountain waters" are surrounded by an orange-sunset vibe. The pools are more spacious than those in Banff, and there are often bighorn sheep milling about. ⏱ *2 hr. See p 115.*

6 Sinclair Canyon. With this stunning farewell, Kootenay closes with a bang just shy of the village of Radium Hot Springs. Your car barely sneaks through iron-rich cliffs that are part of the Redwall Fault, and form a dramatic entrance to the Columbia Valley. There's a small roadside pull-off just west of the canyon where you can get out of the car to walk through the giant walls and take photos, which will be

Natives once used the colorful minerals from these cold springs to make paints.

The soothing mineral waters of the Radium Hot Springs Pool.

especially gorgeous at sunset. Watch for bighorn sheep on the roadside. ⏱ *10 min. 1.5km (1 mile) from Radium and 131km (81 miles) from Alberta–British Columbia (and Banff–Kootenay national parks) border in the middle of the highway.*

Day 5

Travel from Banff to Lake Louise, following Day 3 of "Banff in 1 Week," p 19.

Day 6

Hiking Paradise Valley. Rewarding and challenging, this hike starts in Paradise Valley, just south of Lake Louise. You'll take in a long list of highlights, like the "Giant's Staircase," Lake Annette, and gorgeous views of Mt. Temple. It's a 22km (13.6-mile) hike that will take you all day. *See p 145. Trail head: Paradise Valley parking lot 2.5km (1½ miles) south from Lake Louise Rd.*

Day 7

Visit Yoho National Park as described in Day 6 of "Best of Banff in 1 Week," p 19.

Day 8

Camping at Lake O'Hara. Just the mention of Yoho National Park's Lake O'Hara makes die-hard hikers get misty in the eyes. It's also a great first-camping outing, since you access the backcountry campground via a Parks Canada–run bus—meaning you don't have to carry a heavy load and you can camp in comfort. But you must book a campsite well ahead of time. The bus departs daily from a parking lot just off the Trans-Canada Highway at 8:30am, 10:30am, 3:30pm, and 5:30pm, and you must have a reservation. Once you've set up your tent and settled in, hike around the namesake lake for orientation, then head over past Schäffer Lake to beautiful Lake McArthur, a great 2- to 3-hour hike. *See p 108.*

Day 9

Hiking at Lake O'Hara. Few places in the world can rival the stunning scenery, historic trail system, varied landscape, and special charm of this tiny area tucked beneath the Continental Divide.

Sinclair Canyon marks the striking exit out of Kootenay.

A hiker crosses a bridge in Paradise Valley.

Spend your day on the Lake O'Hara Alpine Circuit, one of the best hikes in the entire world. It'll lead you past such glorious sites as the Opabin Plateau, the Yukness Ledges, and Lake Oesa. After taking the bus from just outside Le Relais Day Shelter back to the parking lot (the last bus of the day leaves at 6:30pm), head back to Lake Louise. *See p 108.*

Day 10

Today follows Day 3 of "Banff In 3 Days" (see p 16), but continues past the Icefield Centre and on to the Town of Jasper. Follow Hwy. 93, the Icefields Parkway, north 105km (65 miles) to Jasper townsite. You should have time to squeeze in the outstanding hike to **Wilcox Pass** as well, for a jaw-dropping lookout of the Columbia Icefield. *See p 46.*

Day 11

Tour of Jasper Townsite and Area. Located in an expansive valley on the west bank of the Athabasca River, Jasper's off-season population hovers around 5,000, but blossoms to more than 20,000 in the summer, when university students from across Canada head here for summer jobs and to mingle with the thousands of travelers passing through, turning the somewhat sleepy mountain town into a vibrant destination. The town itself

The Jasper National Park's Information Centre is a great place to get advice and pick up maps and permits.

is quite large, but most visitors will stick to the two main drags, Connaught Drive and Patricia Street. That's where you'll find the good restaurants, shops, and outfitters.

❶ ★ Jasper National Park Information Centre. Stop here to pick up permits, maps, brochures and to have the friendly staff help you make the most of your day. ⏱ *20 min. 500 Connaught Dr.* ☎ *780/852-6176.*

Head west across Connaught Drive (also known as Hwy. 93), continuing through the lights at the junction with Hwy. 16. Take the first right on Whistlers Road, continuing uphill until you reach:

❷ ★ Jasper Skytram. Your quickest and easiest way to the high alpine terrain, this 7-minute gondola ride takes you up 973m (3,192 ft.), just short of the summit of the Whistlers Mountain. From the top, the views of the Athabasca and Miette valleys are stunning. There's a well-marked, though quite steep, 45-minute self-guided trail to the summit of the mountain. Watch for hoary marmots and white-tailed ptarmigan. Lineups can be intense, so try to head there in the morning. ⏱ *90 min. 3km (1¾ miles) south of Jasper on Hwy. 93, turn left/west on the Whistler Mountain Rd. for another 4km (2½ miles).* ☎ *866/850-8726 and 780/852-3093. www.jasperskytram. com Adults $31, kids 5–14 $16. Apr 7–May 18 10am–5pm, May 19–June 22 9:30am–6:30pm; June 23–Aug 29 9am–8pm; Aug 30–Oct 8 10am–5pm.*

Return to Hwy. 93 and head south 21km (13 miles) to the junction with Hwy. 93A, which heads north. Just past the turnoff is:

❸ Athabasca Falls. Known more for its force than its height, this is one of the most impressive waterfalls in the Rockies, where the Athabasca River (the same one born at the Columbia Icefield and the most important river in Jasper National Park) thunders over a layer of hard quartzite and through a narrow limestone gorge. ⏱ *20 min. 25km (15 miles) south of Jasper.*

Continue north on the scenic Hwy. 93A 18km (11 miles) to the Cavell Rd., a narrow and winding mountain road that requires much attention from drivers. At 15km (9½ miles), you'll arrive at the parking lot beneath:

❹ ★★ Mt. Edith Cavell. This is the highest, and arguably the most scenic mountain in all of Jasper, named for a World War I British nurse. The Angel Glacier saddles the northeastern slope and sends a tongue of ice off the cliffside into a milky blue lake. The Path of the Glacier Trail takes you over boulders, shrubbery, pebbles, and sand through a landscape that, less than a century ago, was covered by a glacier. ⏱ *45 min. Follow Hwy. 93A to the Cavell Rd. Continue another 12km (7½ miles) to the parking lot.*

Take the Cavell Rd. back to Hwy. 93A. Turn left and continue 5.2km (3¼ miles) to the junction with Hwy. 93. Turn left and drive north into the Town of Jasper. Park your car next to the Heritage Railway Station. Cross Connaught Drive and walk up Miette Avenue to Patricia Street.

❺ ★ Coco's Café. Where laid-back locals come to grab lunch, this busy little joint on Patricia Street has yummy wraps, curries, and soups that make superb lunches. There's also great cappuccino, latte, and espresso. The cafe is small and can be cramped; expect to literally rub elbows with your neighbors. *608 Patricia St.* ☎ *780/852-4550. www.cocoscafe.ca. $*

Mt. Edith Cavell, Jasper's tallest mountain.

6 ★ Patricia Street. Now that you've seen the major highlights south and west of town, spend the afternoon strolling the charming shops of Jasper's main streets. Focus on Patricia Street between Hazel Avenue and Cedar Street, then loop back along Connaught Drive. Slow down, enjoy the expansive views, and pick up a souvenir or two. **Counter Clockwise Emporium** (616 Patricia St.; ☎ 780/852-3152) has everything from books and jewelry to soaps and furniture.

Walking back towards your car, cross Connaught Drive at Miette Avenue and pop into the:

7 Heritage Railway Station. Now housing the park administration offices as well as a train station, you can still picture Victorian ladies with their parasols and elaborate dresses mixing with rough 'n' tumble gold diggers at this old frontier outpost. Trains heading east and west across Canada, including the VIA Rail passenger trains, stop here daily. It's still a hub. ○ *10 min. On Connaught Dr. across from Whistlers' Hotel.*

8 Old Fort Point. Jutting out into the Athabasca River, the point offers great views that take in Jasper Townsite, Lac Beauvert, and the Fairmont Jasper Park Lodge. From here you can also catch sight of

Mounts Kerkeslin and Hardisty to the southeast, and the snowy triangle of Mount Edith Cavell, shining above all others, to the south. It's a 2-hour hike atop a glacier-carved knoll to complete the loop via the lookout. Hike counter-clockwise for a gentler climb. ○ *2 hr. To access Old Fort Point, drive 5 min. south of Jasper Townsite via Hwy. 93A and Old Fort Point Rd.* See p 105.

Day 12
The Maligne Valley is a classic glacier-carved hanging valley and a natural wonderland. Have your camera ready—it's also a prime wildlife-viewing spot. Watch for moose, bighorn sheep, bears, and caribou!

Take Connaught Drive east out of town until it joins with Hwy. 16, the Yellowhead Highway. Continue 4km (2½ miles) east to the bridge over the Athabasca River. Turn right. This is the beginning of the Maligne Valley Road.

1 ★★ Maligne Canyon. A waterfall in slow motion, this limestone canyon is at the lip of the Maligne Valley as it meets the much lower Athabasca Valley. There is a lovely series of bridges and walkways that bring you close up to the largest underground drainage system known in Canada. At some points it's only 2m (6.5 ft.) across and 50m (164 ft.) deep! Starting at the upper bridge allows you to see the main highlights. Keep right at all intersections of the self-guided interpretive trail, and then loop back up. ⏱ *30 min. At km 7 (mile 4½) on Maligne Valley Rd.*

Continue south on the Maligne Valley Road until you reach:

❷ **Medicine Lake.** This could be called Mystery Lake—with no visible drainage, this lake seems to evaporate into nothing. The early Natives believed this mysterious lake had healing powers, hence the name. ⏱ *10 min. At km 21 (mile 13) on the Maligne Valley Rd.*

Continue south on the Maligne Valley Road until you reach:

❸ **kids ★★ Maligne Lake Cruise Spirit Island.** A 90-minute cruise on a glass-bottomed boat to a tiny, precious island, dotted with a handful of skinny pines and tucked in a placid corner of this glorious lake (the largest lake in Jasper National Park and the second largest glacial lake in the world), is a great outing for families. The island itself is shrouded in mystery and legends, which the guides

explain en route. From the deck, watch for eagles, mountain goats, and even the odd avalanche, if it's the right time of year. ⏱ *90 min. At km 45 (mile 28) on the Maligne Valley Rd.* ☎ *800/625-4463. www.maligne lake.com Adults $67, kids 5–14 $34. Daily departures hourly from boat docks: thaw date June 4 10am–3pm, June 5–June 30 and Sept 1–Oct 4 10am–4pm, July 1–Aug 31 10am–5pm.*

Return north on the Maligne Valley Road. Just before the Athabasca River bridge, turn left on Old Lodge Road. You'll pass lakes Annette and Edith before arriving at:

❹ **★★ Fairmont Jasper Park Lodge.** The largest commercial property in the Canadian Rocky Mountain National Parks, this classic wilderness lodge attracts tourists and dignitaries from around the world. Hike the hour-long walk around Lac Beauvert, rent a canoe for a paddle on the lake, enjoy a meal at one of the hotel's six restaurants, or play a round on the award-winning golf course. ⏱ *60 min. 3.2km (2 miles) west of Maligne Valley Rd on Old Lodge Rd.* ☎ *780/852-3301. www.fairmont.com/jasper.*

Jasper's Heritage Railway Station transports visitors back in time.

You'll find spectacular views at the award-winning golf course at Fairmont Jasper Park Lodge.

5 Tea at the "JPL". More cozy and casual than its sister hotels (the Banff Springs and the Chateau Lake Louise), tea here is likewise comfortable and delectable, with elegant sandwiches and pastries to accompany more than a dozen teas. Served daily between 2 and 4:30pm in the Emerald Lounge, overlooking Lac Beauvert, Mt. Edith Cavell, and the Whistlers Mountain. *Old Lodge Rd.* 780/852-3301. *$$*

Day 13
kids Rafting on Athabasca River. Choose between a family-friendly scenic float trip on the Athabasca River or Class III on the Sunwapta River. (Sunwapta is a Stoney Indian word meaning "turbulent river"). The big rapid is known as "the Whopper." *611 Patricia St.* 780/852-2665. *www.jasperrafttours.com. Jasper Raft Tours departs for the river daily at 12pm from their office on Patricia St. Adults $65; kids 15–17 $20, 5–14 $10, 4 and under $5.*

If rafting isn't up your alley, book a round at the **Fairmont Jasper Park Lodge's 18-hole course.** (4km/2½ miles east of Jasper Townsite on Hwy. 16, then south on Maligne Lake Rd. and a quick left/west after the bridge, follow 3.2km/2 miles to end; 780/852-6090; www.fairmont.com/jasper/golf; $149–$199; tee times daily 7am–6pm).

Day 14
Grab breakfast at **Bear's Paw** (see p 127; 610 Connaught Dr; the original is still at 4 Cedar Ave.; 780/852-3233; www.bearspawbakery.com). If you are heading back to Banff, drive south along the Icefields Parkway, retracing your steps. It's 287km (178 miles) or 3½ hours if you don't stop, but you'll likely discover the drive equally intriguing and beautiful in a southerly direction. Plan to stop for some photographing and leg-stretching. If you are heading to Edmonton, which is 370km (230 miles) and about 4 hours east, plan to stop for a soak at the Miette Hot Springs en route. See p 102. ●

Banff **for Photographers**

DAY 1

1 Lake Minnewanka
2 Vermillion Lakes
3 Mt. Norquay Road
4 Surprise Corner
5 Eddie Burger + Bar
6 Cascade Gardens
7 Castle Mountain
8 Kootenay Parkway

DAY 2

9 Lake Louise
10 Moraine Lake
11 Trailhead Café
12 Herbert Lake
13 Peyto Lake

Previous page: Bighorn sheep are a common sight in Banff National Park.

Banff National Park is one of the most photographed places in the entire world. Even amateur shutterbugs will be delighted here, where each turn brings another postcard-worthy view. Focusing in on the ultimate photo ops involves timing, patience, and flexibility. But if you get up early, and follow these stops, you'll surely gather a series of award-winners.

Day 1

Head out of Banff on Banff Avenue, going northeast towards Cascade Mountain. Cross under the Trans-Canada Hwy. 1 and continue on:

❶ **Minnewanka Road.** The easiest place for morning wildlife sightings is this drive just northeast of Banff. Watch for bighorn sheep near Two Jack Lake. A photo of Lake Minnewanka in a storm can be extremely dramatic.

Continue to the Trans-Canada Highway and take the westbound ramp. Continue to the second Banff exit. Turn right (west) on Vermillion Lakes Road and continue to where the road ends.

❷ **Mt. Rundle from Vermillion Lakes.** The stillness of the morning on these shallow lakes often brings birdlife and moose. Evening often offers alpine glow on the ridges of Rundle, that unforgettable peak that may be the most famous in all of Banff. In the summer, you can paddle into the middle of the lake for an undisturbed shot—or skate out on the frozen lakes in the winter for an icy masterpiece.

Take a left at Mt. Norquay Road.

❸ **Mt. Norquay Road.** For a great shot that takes in all of the Town of Banff, as well as its scenic surroundings, head up the switchbacks of the Norquay Road to the turnoff.

Drive back into Banff along Mt. Norquay Road, which turns into Gopher Street and then becomes Lynx Street. Turn left at Buffalo Street and continue past Banff Avenue. After the housing ends, the forest thickens. At the next main switchback, park and get out of the car.

❹ **Surprise Corner.** At an elbow bend on the edge of Tunnel Mountain, this is the classic viewpoint for admiring the Fairmont Banff Springs Hotel in all its glory. Sulphur Mountain forms the backdrop, and the majestic Bow Falls rumble beneath. Keep an eye out for fellow photographers crossing the street!

Mt. Rundle may be the most famous peak in Banff.

Cascade Gardens with Cascade Mountain on the horizon.

Head back into town on Buffalo Street and turn left at Banff Avenue.

5️⃣ Lunch at Eddie Burger + Bar. You're hungry and on a tight schedule. For a quick, hearty lunch, you can't beat the homemade burgers at this small joint on Caribou. (See p 71.) *137C Banff Ave. (on Caribou St.).* 📞 *403/762-2230. www.eddieburgerbar.ca. $$*

Follow Banff Avenue over the Bow River Bridge. Take a left at the end of the bridge and a quick right into the parking lot.

6️⃣ Cascade Gardens. At the far end of Banff Avenue, these landscaped gardens provide a great perspective on the hustle and bustle, not to mention the stunning background, of Banff's main drag. Cascade Mountain rises like a pyramid in the distance. Walk from the parking lot to a lookout across the Bow River Bridge. The gardens are open all day June through September and are free to visit.

Drive back out of town, take the Mt. Norquay Road, and then turn left (west) at the Trans-Canada Hwy. 1. The views begin from about 10km (6¼ miles) west of Banff.

7️⃣ Castle Mountain. There are plenty of wonderful angles for capturing the many fine details of this beast of a mountain, between Banff and Lake Louise. With the Bow River in your foreground, you'll capture a dazzling riot of colors. Catch the late afternoon light from the west side of the Vermillion Pass, towards the British Columbia border from Castle Junction.

Turn west on Hwy. 93 towards Radium Hot Springs.

8️⃣ The Kootenay Parkway. Hwy. 93 runs from Castle Junction to Radium Hot Springs in British Columbia, through Kootenay National Park. This is prime wildlife-viewing territory, particularly at dusk. White-tailed deer, bear, moose, coyotes, bighorn sheep, and mountain goats can all be seen. Key spots are at Moose Meadows picnic area, the Inkpots near Hector Gorge, and the stretch between Crooks Meadows and Kootenay Crossing.

Day 2
From the Town of Banff, head west on the Trans-Canada Hwy. 1 58km (36 miles) to Lake Louise. Turn off the highway and head up Lake Louise Road to the famous lake.

1️⃣ Lake Louise. Beautifully framed by tall peaks, with a shimmering surface and a glacier at the back, there's no wonder it's the most photographed lake in Canada. Come here mid-morning for the best light. In winter, that means between 10am and noon. In summer, aim for a 8:30am start for a shot including the boat docks.

Head down 2.5km (1½ miles) on Lake Louise Road, turning right on the Moraine Lake Road and following it for 13km (8 miles).

Photographing Wildlife

Depending on the time of year and your luck, you'll see a wide range of wildlife while roaming Banff National Park with your camera. June is ideal for black bears, late fall is good for bull elks and moose. It's important, though, to respect park rules and always maintain a safe viewing distance from the animals. Usually, this means at least 30m (98 ft.), but for big animals like moose and bear, keep at least 100m (328 ft.) away.

2 Moraine Lake. I've seen the image of this pristine lake on everything from the former $10 bill to a beer advertisement. The Valley of the Ten Peaks in the background oozes with drama. Come before noon.

Retrace your route and turn right on Lake Louise Road, returning to Lake Louise village.

3 Trailhead Café. Pick up lunch to go at this busy little cafe in Samson Mall. Grab a fresh wrap—there are more than a dozen to choose from, but I love the tropical wrap with chicken and mango salsa, or the donair wrap with lamb. They pack up nice and clean for a picnic later on. *In Samson Mall.* ☎ *403/522-2006.* $

Head west on the Trans-Canada Highway and then north on the Icefields Parkway towards Jasper to 2.5km (1½ miles) north of the Icefield Parkway gate.

4 Herbert Lake. Because this lake is both small and sheltered by the tall peaks around it, it provides glass-like reflection in the morning, with the sun shining on the Bow Range in front, as well as Mt. Bosworth to the north or Mt. Temple and the peaks of Lake Louise to the south.

Continue north on the Icefields Parkway another 39km (24 miles).

5 Peyto Lake. With a blue deeper than the waters of the Caribbean, and steep edges of mountain all around, Peyto Lake is a must-stop on the Icefields Parkway. In July and August, wildflowers are blooming. It's well worth the short stroll to the lookout.

Few Banff visitors leave without a breathtaking photograph of Lake Louise.

Banff with Kids

DAY 1

1. Banff Gondola
2. Banff Park Museum
3. Sushi House
4. Biking on the Sundance Trail or Golf Course Loop
5. Fairmont Banff Springs Hotel
6. Grizzly House
7. Evening Interpretive Theatre

DAY 2

8. Hiking to Boom Lake

DAY 3

9. Lake Louise Sightseeing Gondola
10. Bill Peyto's Café
11. Glacier Adventure

Legend:

- △ Campground
- ⛽ Gasoline
- ⓘ Information
- Ⓟ Parking
- ■ Point of Interest

Families flock to Banff for adventure, nature, and quality time surrounded by inspiring fresh air. Lifelong mountain lovers are born here every day—just ask the locals, most of whom first fell for these peaks on a family vacation. The keys to keeping kids engaged include getting out of the car a lot, following your nose with a sense of adventure and discovery, and keeping track of all that you see and learn. Be sure to pick up Parks Canada's excellent "Xplorers" workbook for kids, which is full of fun activities and ways to discover the park. It's available at all Visitor Information Centres.

Day 1

Drive south on Banff Avenue, over the Bow River Bridge. Turn left and then right quickly onto Mountain Road. Follow until it ends at:

1 Banff Gondola. This may be your child's first summit, and the thrill won't soon be forgotten. After the 8-minute gondola ride drops you on top of the world, hike the 700 steps, across a secure boardwalk, to the top of Samson's Peak. ⏱ *90 min. See p 13.*

Head back down Mountain Avenue, turning left onto Spray Road and right over the Bow River Bridge. Take a quick left onto Buffalo Street, then turn left into the parking lots between Central Park and:

2 Banff Park Museum National Historic Site. Kids will like the discovery room inside this natural history museum, which is inside a log building built in 1903.

Hundreds of wildlife species are on display at the Banff Park Museum.

With more than 5,000 species of birds, insects, and wildlife on display, it's a one-stop shop for learning about the Rockies. Great on a rainy day. ⏱ *45 min. See p 52.*

You can leave your car parked next to the museum. Walk up Banff Avenue, turning right at Caribou Street. Half a block later, on your left-hand side is:

3 Sushi House. Family-friendly restaurants are a dime-a-dozen in Banff. But adventurous kids will love to choose selections of sushi off a model train carrying the food around the eating counter at the tiny Sushi House. Each dish is priced according to the color of the plate—and just ask the sushi master inside the tracks if there's something special you'd like. The food is fresh and healthy, and the atmosphere is convivial and fun. *304 Caribou St.* ☎ *403/762-4353. $.*

Walk to the west end of Caribou Street, turning left on Bear Street for:

4 Biking. Kids love to try new things. Rent a bike in Banff and head up the Sundance Trail towards Sundance Canyon. The 3.7km (2.3-mile) trail has little elevation gain and is paved the entire way. Another option good for families is the 15km (9⅓-mile) Golf Course Loop. It's peaceful and pretty. Banff Adventures (211 Bear St.; ☎ 403/762-4554;

At Sushi House, diners select dishes that are delivered via a model railroad.

www.banffadventures.com) rents kids' bikes, trailers, and strollers.

After dropping off your bikes, return to your car. Drive back over the Bow River Bridge, taking a left onto Spray Road. Follow it until it ends at:

⑤ The "Castle in the Rockies." Little girls will love to put on a party dress and explore inside the utterly distinctive Fairmont Banff Springs Hotel. Before you settle in for an English-style tea, roam medieval corridors and wander through luxurious ballrooms. ⏱ *90 min. 405 Spray Ave.* ☎ *403/762-6860. www.fairmont. com/banff. Tea in the Rundle Lounge $42 for adults, $18 for children 6–12.*

From Banff Avenue, turn east or right on Wolf Street, then northeast or left on Tunnel Mountain Road. Drive 4km (2½ miles) to the

Enjoying a family-friendly bike route.

entrance to Tunnel Mountain Campground.

⑥ Grizzly House. Mixing Gilligan's island with Heidi's alpine shack, there is loads of personality here. It's noisy and raucous, great for energetic families. The specialties are cheese or beef fondues, but the most exotic version has you hot-dipping shark, alligator, rattlesnake, ostrich, and frogs legs. *207 Banff Ave.* ☎ *403/762-4055. www. banffgrizzlyhouse.com. $$.*

⑦ Evening Interpretive Theater. Nature interpreters from Banff National Park offer a variety of evening activities at the Tunnel Mountain Theatre, inside the Tunnel Mountain Campground. Throughout the summer, there are daily programs at 7:30pm, ranging from a historical rendition of Banff's legendary characters to stories of adventure in the peaks. They're fun, participatory, a great learning experience. Best of all, they're free! ⏱ *45 min. Contact Parks Canada for updated schedules at* ☎ *403/762-1550.*

Day 2
Grab a picnic lunch, your bear spray, some water, sunscreen, and your rain gear, and hit the trails. Drive west from Banff on the Trans-Canada Hwy. 1 (28km/17 miles) to

Castle Junction. Turn west onto Hwy. 93A S.

8 Hiking to Boom Lake.

Scores of life-long hikers have had their first thrills on the trail here in Banff. There are many kid-friendly hikes to choose from. I suggest the relatively gentle climb to Boom Lake, which is surrounded by a massive limestone wall along the Continental Divide. The trail has a real sense of discovery to it. Bring a picnic—it's a 10km (6.2-mile) return trip that will take you 4 hours or so. *Trail head is off Hwy. 93 S., 7km (4 miles) west of Castle Junction.*

Day 3

Head out of Banff, west on the Trans-Canada Hwy. 1 (58km/36 miles) to the turnoff for Lake Louise. Turn right, heading up the hill to:

1 Lake Louise Sightseeing Gondola.

Kids are both scared and intrigued by grizzly bears, and this is a superb place to learn more about the often-misunderstood beast that rules the Banff backcountry. Interpretive guides explain how the "grizz" makes its home. ⏱ *2 hr. See p 62.*

Drive down the hill, over the Trans-Canada Hwy. 1. At the main intersection, turn right on Village Road right past Samson Mall. Past the red-roofed Post Hotel, take a left into the entrance for:

2 Bill Peyto's Café.

Located inside the Lake Louise Hostel and Alpine Centre, the food here is healthy, creative, and priced for most budgets. The timber-framed room with a stone fireplace makes for a relaxed, friendly atmosphere. Service is fast. Try the bison burgers, the Alberta beef chili, or the Alpine club sandwich. There's also a kids' menu. *In the Lake Louise Hostel and Alpine Centre. 203 Village Rd.* ☎ *403/522-2200. www.hihostels.ca and search on "Bill Peyto's." $.*

Exit Lake Louise, turning west or left onto the Trans-Canada Hwy. 1. Turn north on Hwy. 93, the Icefields Parkway, continuing for 130km (81 miles) until you reach:

3 The Glacier Adventure.

Hop on a giant tractor-like bus called a "snocoach" with sky-high wheels, drive onto a frozen tongue of ice, and then hike out on the ice– not your average day in the park. Tours leave every 15 minutes or so and can be combined with a visit to the Glacier Skywalk glass-bottomed platform. It's best to visit the icefield in the mornings or late afternoon to avoid the throngs of tourists arriving by bus from the towns of Banff and Jasper. *Tour lasts* ⏱ *90 min. See p 17.*

This "snocoach" takes adventurous tourists into the Icefields.

Banff in Wintertime

△	Campground
⛽	Gasoline
✚	Hospital/First Aid
ⓘ	Information
▪	Point of Interest

DAY 1
1 Mt. Norquay
2 Sleigh ride

DAY 2
3 Ice skating
4 Cross-country skiing
5 Waldhaus

DAY 3
6 Ski Lake Louise

DAY 4
7 Puppy Power
8 Spa Power
9 NHL Hockey

DAY 5
10 Sunshine Village

0   10 mi
0   10 km

Banff becomes a winter wonderland from late November through early April. Famous for its crisp blue skies, winter in the Canadian Rockies is just as beautiful as summer. In fact, many people swear that winter is an even better time to visit. For those not hindered by the cold, skiing in Banff is a one-of-a-kind experience. And don't forget all those snowmen and women waiting to be built and evening strolls waiting to be taken under star-studded skies, often active with the stunning *aurora borealis* ("northern lights").

Day 1

❶ Alpine Skiing at Mt Norquay. A week is just barely enough to sample the best the area has to offer. Together, the three ski resorts in Banff—Mt. Norquay, Sunshine Village, and Ski Louise—make this one of the great ski destinations in North America. I recommend visiting them each for at least a day. For Day 6, you could return to whichever you liked best (and that's an endless debate that rages on in Banff and will give you plenty to chat to folks about on the chairlift!). The SkiBig 3 partnership sells a package to all three (☎ 877/754-7080 or 403/762-4561; www.skibig3.com).Guided experiences include ski coaching, insider terrain, and passes to all three resorts. **Mt. Norquay** is a locals' favorite because it's intimate and less than 15 minutes from Banff Avenue. There are plenty of intermediate runs, and it

makes a good half-day. Economical ski-by-the-hour deals are good for lighter days. ☎ *403/762-4421. www.banffnorquay.com. See p 157.*

Evening 1

❷ Sleigh Ride. For a romantic winter evening, snuggle up under a cozy blanket with someone special, join a cowboy, and head out for a one-horse open-sleigh ride with Banff Trail Riders. *132 Banff Ave. ☎ 403/762-4551. www.horseback. com. Adults $32, children 4-12 $27.*

Day 2

❶ Ice Skating. There are a number of places where you can skate outdoors under the winter sky. It's an exhilarating activity that's popular with families. Try the Vermillion Lakes, just outside the Town of Banff, in the early winter before the snow starts to pile up. Take Mt. Norquay Road out of town, turning

Skating on Vermillion Lake.

Cross-country skiing just before sunset.

left on Vermillion Lakes Drive just before the Trans-Canada Hwy. 1. You can rent skates in Banff at **Snowtips** (225 Bear St.; ☎ 403/762-8177; www.snowtips-bactrax.com; from $14/day). At the Fairmont Chateau Lake Louise, there is an outdoor rink on the lake with a spectacular ice castle built right on top. It's a very scenic and romantic place to skate. *At the top of Lake Louise Dr. Rent skates at Chateau Mountain Sports inside the hotel.* ☎ 403/522-3837. www.chateau mountainsports.com. From $13 for 2 hr. or $16/day.

❷ Cross-Country Skiing. A wonderful way to explore the park in winter, cross-country (or "Nordic") skiing promises great exercise, views—and solitude, if you're seeking it. There are more than 80km (50 miles) of managed trails in Banff National Park, many of them within a half-hour drive of Banff Townsite. The cross-country ski season runs from December to March. Try the Spray River Loop, which departs from the parking lot at Bow Falls, and the Shoreline Trail at Lake Louise, which starts just in front of the Chateau Lake Louise. See p 158 for ski-rental information.

❸ On a crisp winter night, your cheeks aglow from a day in the mountains, what could be more divine than a steaming pot of Alpine-inspired fondue? The best fondue in Banff is at the **Waldhaus,** a Bavarian-style cottage in the woods beneath the Fairmont Banff Springs Hotel. *405 Spray Ave.* ☎ 403/762-6860. www.fairmont. com/banff. See p 79. $$$.

Day 3
Ski Lake Louise. For jaw-dropping views, coupled with an incredibly varied terrain, head to this legendary ski resort across the valley from its famed namesake lake. Be sure to drop by cozy Temple Lodge for lunch. Nonskiers can go snowshoeing or on a guided wildlife tour. ☎ 800/258-7669 or 403/522-3555. www.skilouise.com. See p 157.

Day 4
❶ Puppy Power. It's one of the oldest forms of transportation in the world. Dog sledding is offered just outside Banff in Kananaskis Country. Drive the dogs or just ride

Dog sledding is one of the oldest forms of transportation in the world.

You Are in Avalanche Country

The Canadian Rockies is avalanche country. An extremely powerful wave of snow and ice that cracks off a mountain slope, an avalanche can destroy everything in its path. It's extremely challenging to predict when an avalanche might occur, and even more challenging to escape if you are caught in one. Drivers should avoid stopping in areas where Parks Canada has posted an AVALANCHE ZONE sign. Parks Canada updates avalanche forecasts regularly throughout the winter. In Banff, call ☎ 403/762-1460.

along as you mush your way across a frozen lake. *Book through Snowy Owl Tours.* ☎ *403/678-4369. www. snowyowltours.com. 104-602 Bow Valley Parkway, Canmore. $159–$667 per person.*

❷ **Spa Power.** Work off all those kinks with a visit to the private and decadent **Willowstream Spa** at the Fairmont Banff Hot Springs. After soaking in the mineral pools, indulge in a mountain stone massage or an après-ski massage. *405 Spray Ave.* ☎ *800/404-1772 or 403/762-2211. www.fairmont.com/ banff-springs/willow-stream. From $189 for 60 min.*

Evening 3 or 4
❸ **NHL Hockey.** Hockey is a fast-paced game, and you'll catch some of the world's best ice hockey players in action at the Calgary Saddledome, cheering on the NHL's Calgary Flames. Pure Canadiana! *Book through Banff Adventures (*☎ *403/762-4554; www.banff adventures.com; from $115/person),* which has shuttles from Banff for all Flames home games.

Day 5
Sunshine Village. Tucked along the Continental Divide, beautiful Sunshine Village generally has the best snow, lots of good intermediate

runs, and the notoriously extreme Delirium Dive, for experts only. Sunshine also has the best terrain park in the area and magnificent views of Mt. Assiniboine. Even better, spend the night at Sunshine Mountain Lodge and get first turns in the morning. ☎ *800/661-1676 or 403/762-6500. www.skibanff.com. See p 157.*

Skiing through fresh powder at Sunshine Village.

Glaciers & Wildlife

GLACIERS

1 Mt. Temple
2 Mt. Victoria
3 Bath Glacier
4 Crowfoot Glacier
5 Bow Glacier
6 Snowbird Glacier
7 Saskatchewan Glacier
8 Columbia Icefield
9 Athabasca Glacier
10 Snow Dome

WILDLIFE

11 Urban Elk in Town of Banff
12 Minnewanka Loop
13 Muleshoe
14 Bourgeau Wildlife Overpass
15 Helen Lake
16 Bow Summit
17 Waterfowl Lakes
18 Mt. Coleman

0   10 mi
0   10 km

Gasoline
Hospital/First Aid
Information
Point of Interest
Skiing

Studying the cycles of nature in the incredible mountain wilderness of the Canadian Rockies is enlightening, astounding, and inspiring. There are more than 1,000 glaciers in Banff, and all of them are retreating. Scientists say the glaciers of Banff lost 25% of their mass during the 20th century. Most can't be seen from the convenience of the major highways. There is, however, an easy-to-access and varied selection you can spot from the roadside, ranging from almost-hidden glaciers like the Snowbird to the most famous glacier in North America, the Athabasca.

Travel Tip

Most of these glaciers are northeast facing, so the light will be better for seeing them in the first half of the day.

Glaciers in Banff National Park

1 Mt. Temple. This may be my favorite peak in Banff. With a giant pyramid-like shape and a beautiful glacier below its summit, Mt. Temple dominates the horizon south of Lake Louise. *6km (3¾ miles) east of Lake Louise on Trans-Canada Hwy. 1.*

2 Mt. Victoria. One of the most photographed mountains in the world, this wide peak provides the scenic backdrop to Lake Louise. Always snow covered, it's best appreciated from the 5.3km (3.3-mile) hike to the Plain of the Six Glaciers, where the Aberdeen, Upper Lefroy, Lower Lefroy, Upper Victoria, Lower Victoria, and Pope's glaciers (as seen left to right or southeast to southwest) are all

visible. It's a 4-hour round-trip that departs on the shore of Lake Louise just past the Fairmont Chateau Lake Louise, heading to the right around the lake. *See p 144.*

3 Bath Glacier. Part of the mighty Waputik Icefield, the Bath Glacier hugs the mid-ridge of Mt. Daly. It can be seen at Mt. Hector, just north of Lake Louise. *17km (11 miles) north of Lake Louise on Hwy. 93.*

4 Crowfoot Glacier. Years ago, there were three toe-like extensions of this glacier clinging to the side of a cliff. The lowest "toe" has retreated completely, leaving a rare two-toed crow. *32km (20 miles) north of Lake Louise on Hwy. 93.*

5 Bow Glacier. Visible at the back of the valley behind Num-Ti-Jah Lodge, the Bow Glacier is the same glacier that originally carved out the entire Bow Valley (which you've driven through as you came northwest from Banff) 10,000 years

Upper Bow Lake with the Bow Glacier in the background.

Hiking on Parker Ridge with the Saskatchewan Glacier in the background.

ago. For a closer view, hike the 4.6km (2.9-mile) trail to Bow Glacier Falls, which starts just behind Num-Ti-Jah Lodge. *36km (22 miles) north of Lake Louise on Hwy. 93.*

❻ Snowbird Glacier. Clinging to the east face of Mt. Patterson, just north of Bow Pass, the beautiful Snowbird Glacier drapes over a cliff, with wings that are limited in size by the width of each ledge. Only the left wing is visible from the highway, best seen 3.1km (2 miles) north of the Silverhorn Creek Bridge, on the west side of the highway at the bottom of the hill past Bow Summit. *48km (30 miles) north of Lake Louise on Hwy. 93.*

❼ Saskatchewan Glacier. The longest tongue of ice flowing off the Columbia Icefield, this is a

Tourists explore the Columbia Icefield.

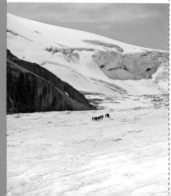

classic outlet valley glacier. The best view is from Parker Ridge, a superb 2.7km (1.7-mile) hike up the ridge from the highway. *117km (73 miles) north of Lake Louise on Hwy. 93. See p 148.*

❽ Columbia Icefield. The largest frozen ice mass south of the Arctic Circle, this icefield measures 325 sq. km (125 sq. miles). It includes six glaciers: Athabasca, Saskatchewan, Dome, Columbia, Castleguard, and Stutfield. *125km (78 miles) north of Lake Louise on Hwy. 93. See p 99 for more information on experiencing the Icefield.*

❾ Athabasca Glacier. The most famous glacier in North America is in Jasper National Park. It's also the easiest glacier to access—more than 10,000 people visit this frozen river of ice each busy summer day. *125km (78 miles) north of Lake Louise on Hwy. 93. See p 99.*

❿ Snow Dome. Also in Jasper National Park, this peak is a hydrological apex. One of only two in the world, water flows in three directions: north to the Arctic Ocean, east to the Atlantic Ocean, and west to the Pacific Ocean. The Dome Glacier can be seen on Snowdome's north side as you approach the Columbia Icefield from the north on Hwy. 93.

Banff is no zoo! Here, animals roam free, and the natural rhythms of the wilderness are maintained. There are 53 species of wild mammals in Banff, 13 of which are on Parks Canada's "Species at Risk" list. Count yourself lucky if you catch any wildlife sightings in Banff. But if you follow this list, your chances will be higher. Dawn and dusk are the best times of day for spotting wildlife. Be sure to keep track, and report all wildlife sightings to Parks Canada at ☎ 403/762-1470.

Wildlife in Banff National Park

❶ Urban Elk in Town of Banff. During certain times of the year (mainly spring and summer), elk make their way into the heart of the Town of Banff. The drive around the Banff Springs Golf Course is a prime area for spotting these magnificent mammals. *At the end of Golf Course Dr. past Bow Falls.*

❷ Minnewanka Loop. Just northeast of the Town of Banff, the drive along the Minnewanka Road is particularly good for seeing bighorn sheep who often gather near Two Jack Lake, 12km (7½ miles) from Town of Banff on Minnewanka Loop. *Take Banff Ave to the northeast out of town. It turns into Minnewanka Loop after going under the Trans-Canada Hwy.*

❸ Muleshoe. An open pasture off the Bow Valley Parkway Hwy. 1A, this is a good spot for coyotes, elk, and mule deer. Birders also come here to spot Western Tanagers and Hammond's flycatchers. *Take the Trans-Canada Hwy. 1 (5.5km/3½ miles) west of Banff to the Bow Valley Pkwy. Hwy. 1A. Continue for 5.5km (3½ miles) to Muleshoe Picnic Area.*

❹ Bourgeau Wildlife Overpass. This is one of six specially designed tree-covered bridges that go over the Trans-Canada Hwy. 1 west of Banff and allow wildlife like bears, elk, coyotes, wolves, cougars, and moose to roam freely in their natural habitat. They're aimed at reducing the large number of mammals (and humans) that were being killed by vehicles, and

A bull elk crosses the Bow River.

Bear Jams: Keep Moving, People!

Everybody's thrilled to catch a glimpse of a bear in the wild. In the Canadian Rockies, there are more "bear jams" than "traffic jams" as tourists pile up in their vehicles to snap photos of grizzlies or black bears, creating chaos on the roads. Whistling, yelling, running about . . . tourists behave strangely in the presence of a magnificent mammal, causing problems that can turn fatal for the bear and for other drivers. If you see a bear and want a closer look, slow down safely but do not stop. Give the bear space. The moment one car stops, everybody stops. No matter the circumstances, stay in your vehicle and do not approach the bear. Once alerted to the sighting of a bear, Parks Canada staff and often the police will appear at the scene and urge travelers to keep moving. Remember to call in a bear sighting to ☎ 403/762-1470.

they've been extremely successful. There are also 38 underpasses between Banff and Lake Louise. A small but smart interpretive display can be visited at the Hwy. 1 Castle viewpoint rest area located just 1.5 km (1 mile) west of the Redearth Creek trailhead, another 9.5 km (6 miles) past the Bourgeau Overpass. *11km (6¾ miles) northwest of Banff on the Trans-Canada Hwy. 1.*

5 Helen Lake. From the high alpine environment of this hiking

Keep your eyes peeled for mountain goats.

trail near the Crowfoot Glacier, you'll be tramping through prime grizzly bear habitat, and may also spot white-tailed ptarmigan, grouse, and golden eagles. *33km (21 miles) north of Lake Louise on the Icefields Pkwy. See p 147.*

6 Bow Summit. Following the short interpretive trail to the Peyto Lake and on to the Bow Summit lookout, you may be able to see cute little mammals like pikas (which look like miniature rabbits) and hoary marmots. *41km (25 miles) north of Lake Louise on the Icefields Pkwy.*

7 Waterfowl Lakes. You won't be surprised to see mallard ducks and loons on these lakes. What may well surprise you, however, is spotting a moose. Summer evenings are the best time. *58km (36 miles) north of Lake Louise on the Icefields Pkwy.*

8 Mt. Coleman. From the picnic area at its base, mountain goats can be spotted clinging precariously to the cliff of this peak. *100km (62 miles) north of Lake Louise on the Icefields Pkwy.* ●

4 Banff National Park

The Town of Banff

0   1/4 mi
0   1/4 km

- - - Walking Path

1 Banff Information Centre
2 Bow River Promenade
3 Central Park
4 Banff Park Museum
5 Cascade Gardens
6 Bow Falls
7 Old Banff homes
8 Nester's Market
9 Whyte Museum
10 Canada House Gallery
11 Cascade Plaza
12 Can. Ski Museum West
13 Banff Avenue
14 Three Ravens Wine Bar
15 The Banff Centre

Previous page: Relaxing by postcard-pretty Moraine Lake.

The Town of Banff is the beating heart of Canada's first and most important national park. Planned and organized as a resort town from the beginning, the focus here remains on pleasing visitors. There are historic and natural highlights dotted around the outskirts of town, but the center of all things is bustling Banff Avenue, the main drag. Here, tourists speaking dozens of languages nip in and out of shops, pop into a pub for a pint, get their skis and bikes tuned up, and enjoy some truly fabulous cuisine.

❶ ★★ Banff Information Centre. This is a must for your first stop of the day. In the heritage building in the heart of "downtown" Banff, it's a great orientation center, with helpful desks staffed by the friendly folks at Parks Canada and the Banff-Lake Louise Tourism Bureau. They have maps, brochures, and trail updates, and they can help you decide what to do when. At the back, there's a short video that will also help you get your bearings and understand just why this place is so important.
⏱ 20 min. 224 Banff Ave. ☎ 403/ 762-1550. Mid-June to early-Sept 9am–7pm, mid-Sept to mid-June 9am–5pm. Closed Dec 25. See p 13.

Exit the Information Centre and cross Banff Avenue at the lights at the corner of Wolf Street. Continue down Wolf Street 3 blocks, crossing Bear and Lynx streets, until you reach:

❷ Bow River Promenade. The canoe docks mark the beginning of a gentle, paved trail that follows one of Canada's most important rivers. The beautiful Bow River is the longest river in Banff National Park. From its headwaters at Bow Lake, 90km (56 miles) north of the Town of Banff, it flows south and east, passing through Banff, Canmore, and Calgary. It joins the South Saskatchewan River and eventually drains into Hudson Bay and the Atlantic Ocean, on Canada's east coast. This promenade makes for a good stroll full of wonderful views.

Follow the trail downriver, around the bend to:

❸ Central Park. Site of Canada Day parties, weddings, picnics, and

A couple enjoys a walk along the Bow River.

Banff's Cascade Gardens.

Frisbee-tossing, this is Banff's main outdoor meeting space. During the summer, Parks Canada's "Roving Interpreters" often set up shop at one of the picnic tables (you'll spot them in their red and green uniforms). Sometimes there are elk feeding here, too! ⏱ *15 min. Along the north shore of the Bow River btw. Banff Ave. and Bow Ave. parallel to Buffalo St.*

Next to the park, on the east side between the park and Banff Avenue, is:

One of Banff's original heritage homes.

④ **kids** ★★ **Banff Park Museum.** A beautiful building dating to 1903 and reflecting early Rocky Mountain architecture, this is the oldest natural history museum in Western Canada. It houses an incredibly complete collection of wildlife. It's also a superb rainy-day option. Come for a good look at beaver's teeth or an elk's antler. Daily tours start at 3pm. ⏱ *30 min. 91 Banff Ave.* ☎ *403/762-1558. Adults $4, seniors $3, youth $2. Free for children 5 and under. July 1–Sept 5 10am–5pm, Sept 6 to mid-Oct Wed–Sun 10am–5pm. Closed mid-Oct to mid-May.*

Walk over the Bow River Bridge. Cross Mountain Road and head through the iron gate for a visit to:

⑤ **Cascade Gardens.** Inspired by the geological history of the Rockies, this lovely garden includes a series of fountains, or "cascades," that are an essential part of appreciating the architecture and design of the Banff Administration Building. During summer, the local Siksika First Nation erects a traditional tepee here with an interesting cultural exhibit. Turn to face Cascade Mountain and Banff Avenue for that timeless photo opportunity.

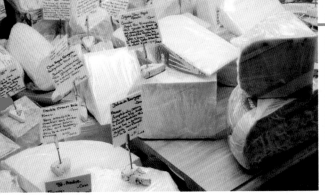

Some of the cheeses available at Nester's Market.

🕐 *30 min. At the T-intersection where Spray and Cave aves. meet Banff Ave., just over the Bow River Bridge. Free admission. Daily 24 hr.*

Back across Mountain Road, turn right (east) before crossing the bridge, following the trail 1.2km (.8 miles) to:

❻ ★ Bow Falls. Tucked in beneath the Fairmont Banff Springs Hotel, Bow Falls will let you escape the hustle and bustle of the busy Banff Townsite. The 10m (33-ft.) falls, eroding between two rock formations, roar and wash away any tension you may have picked up. The rock on the left bank of the river is 245 million years old, while the one on the right bank is some 320 million years old. Downstream from the falls, the Banff Springs Golf Course dominates the southern side of the valley.

Walk back up river. At the Bow River Bridge, take the east (or downriver) sidewalk, and begin exploring the historic neighborhoods of "old Banff," along Beaver and Muskrat streets.

❼ Old Banff homes. Along Buffalo Street, backing onto the Bow River, are some of the most spectacular homes in Western Canada. Remember, Banff has a "need to reside" rule—only people with jobs or businesses in Banff can live here. At 313 Buffalo St. is a home dating to 1920 that was once the Park Superintendent's Residence. At the corner of Buffalo and Muskrat streets, you'll find the historic Grant-Hemming home, built in 1921 from local materials (note the Rundle-stone steps and riverstone chimney). Next door are legendary naturalist and climatologist Norman Sanson's home and the summer residence of Senator Amedée Forget.

❽ If you were drawn to one of the riverside picnic tables along the Bow River, drop into **Nester's Market.** With a deli, bakery, and plenty of fresh produce, you can put together a superb lunch to-go. *122 Bear St.* ☎ *403/762-3663. www.nestersmarket.com/banff. Daily 8am–11pm. $.*

Walk back to the Bow River trail at the end of Muskrat Street, and continue along the river, passing Central Park. On Lynx Street, turn right to:

❾ ★★ Whyte Museum of the Canadian Rockies. This museum houses excellent exhibits about the human history of Banff and has a tremendously wealthy archive of

Banff National Park

The entrance to Banff's Whyte Museum.

memoirs, sketches, photographs, and personal artifacts of Rocky Mountain pioneers, visionaries, and artists. Changing exhibits shine light on how the mountains have inspired generations; the newest is Gateway to the Rockies, which looks at local history with interactive displays. Another excellent rainy-day activity. ⏱ *90 min. 111 Bear St.* ☎ *403/762-2291. www.whyte.org. Adults $8, students $4, free for children under 12. Daily 10am–5pm.*

Cross Lynx Street and head down the lovely Bear Street. On the lefthand side, a few shops down, you'll find:

❿ ★ Canada House Gallery.
Even if you aren't a dedicated art collector, it's worth taking time to explore this fine arts shop and gallery. Featuring exclusively Canadian art, the focus is on landscape, contemporary, and Native styles. It's not hard to understand how the Rockies inspire these artists. There are often opening receptions for the public on Saturday afternoons. ⏱ *20 min. 201 Bear St.* ☎ *403/762-3757. www.canadahouse.com. Sun–Thurs 9:30am–6pm, Fri–Sat 9:30am–7pm.*

The Rockies inspire much of the art at Canada House Gallery.

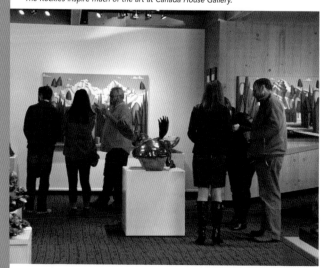

Follow Bear Street to its terminus at Wolf Street and head into:

11 Cascade Plaza. For a quick and affordable pick-me-up, jump into the food court at the basement of Banff's biggest mall. You'll find a dozen different counters serving everything from sushi and pizza to curries. You can buy lunch for under $8. *317 Banff Ave. ☎ 403/762-8484. www.cascadeshops.com. $.*

Before riding the escalators up, start at the bottom floor display for:

12 Canadian Ski Museum West. From early wooden tele-mark skis to the latest World Cup victories, the history of Banff's favorite sport is told in displays throughout the three-story Cascade Mall. Start at the first floor and work your way up to follow in chronological order. You may even bump into a real ski legend or two while roaming about Banff. ⏱ *20 min. 317 Banff Ave. ☎ 403/762-8484. Free admission. Mon–Thurs 10am–8pm, Fri–Sat 10am–9pm, Sun 10am–6pm.*

Exit the mall and turn right to stroll:

13 Banff Avenue. Home to great shops, cafes, restaurants, historic buildings, and a general hustle-and-bustle, take time to stroll the scene and eavesdrop on dozens of languages on one of Canada's iconic main drags. A massive rede-velopment project in 2007 widened the sidewalks and made street life more pleasant.

Head up Wolf Street and turn right on St. Julien Road. Follow the curving road until you enter the campus of the Banff Centre.

An opera performance at the Banff Centre.

14 ★ Three Ravens Wine Bar. For a quick pre-concert bite to eat or a cocktail, or a post-event glass of wine and dessert, you can't beat this scenic restaurant above the Sally Borden Building in the Banff Centre. It wins for the best restau-rant view in Banff, by far. Try a glass of pinot noir from the Okanagan with Spanish paprika beef rolls. *At the Banff Centre on St. Julien Rd. ☎ 403/762-6300. www.banffcentre. ca. Daily 4pm–midnight. $$.*

15 The Banff Centre. Part of the town's fabric for nearly a century, this is a world-renowned arts, cul-ture, and educational institution that hosts celebrated musicians, writers, and other artists from around the world on a regular basis. The Centre's Summer Arts Festival showcases the best in a variety of artistic areas—from cos-tume design and creative writing, to drama and opera, to jazz and classical music. It's another place where the mountains truly awaken inspiration and creativity. Don't miss the chance to take in a truly inspir-ing performance, often in the out-doors, during your visit to Banff. *St. Julien Rd. ☎ 403/762-6100. www. banffcentre.ca.*

Lake Minnewanka

0 ——— 1 mi
0 ——— 1 km

•••• Walking Path

BANFF NATIONAL PARK

Cascade Mountain

Lake Minnewanka Loop

Lake Minnewanka

Two Jack Lake

Banff Ave.

Trans-Canada Highway

Tunnel Mountain Rd.

BANFF

Johnson Lake

start here ★

finish here ★

1. Hoodoos
2. Bankhead
3. Lake Minnewanka
4. Stewart Canyon
5. Johnson Lake

Some call it a giant bathtub, but Lake Minnewanka does offer unique activities and a chance for open skies. It's the biggest lake in Banff National Park, created by nature and later expanded by humanity. The Minnewanka Loop makes a nice tour from the Town of Banff, and can be done in a leisurely 2 or 3 hours. To extend it, add in the hike to C-Level Cirque or another of the hikes listed in chapter 6. Watch for bighorn sheep on the road near Two Jack Lake—and remember not to feed them.

1 Hoodoos. The mysterious pillars look like they've been dropped from outer space. In fact, they are freestanding posts made of silt, gravel, and rocks cemented together by dissolved limestone. The un-cemented particles were slowly eroded and washed away. There is a paved, stroller-friendly 500m (1,640-ft.) trail to a nice viewpoint that also offers lovely views of Mt. Rundle and the Bow River. *Just off Tunnel Mountain Rd. past the entrance to Tunnel Mountain*

Campground Village I, 4km (2½ miles) east of Banff.

Tunnel Mountain Road continues to loop around until it meets up with Lake Minnewanka Road again, which passes under the Trans-Canada Hwy. 1 and goes northeast along the side of Cascade Mountain. Pull off Lake Minnewanka Road after 3km (1¾ miles).

2 Bankhead. Once the working center of Banff, Bankhead was a small settlement that boomed in

Mt. Rundle, the Bow River, and the Hoodoos from the Hoodoo Trail Overlook.

the early 20th century. Old machinery and foundations are still in place, such as the entranceway to the former church and the transformer building, which features a display about coal mining. A short 10-minute walk about the area, following interpretive displays, will help bring the history to life.

Continue down the road another 2.6km (1½ miles) and pull into the large parking lot just before:

❸ **Lake Minnewanka.** This lake used to be called "The Lake of the Water Spirits" by the Stoney Nation, who apparently feared these spirits and refused to swim in or boat on the lake. Early Europeans took a

likewise timid view, calling it "Devil's Lake." Although it's too cold for a dip, boaters today have no fear. This is the only lake in Banff where motorboats are allowed. From May through October, you can take an enclosed boat trip to the end of the lake. 🕐 *60 min.* ☎ *403/762-3473. www.explorerockies.com. Adults $56, children 6–15 $29, free for children 5 and under.*

To the north of the parking lot is a day-use area with picnic tables and shelters. Continue through to reach the trail for Stewart Canyon.

❹ ★ **Stewart Canyon.** A nice 30-minute round-trip walk along the lakeshore takes you to this canyon, named for the first superintendent of Banff National Park. Much of the canyon has lain underwater since Minnewanka was dammed, first in 1895 and again in 1912 and 1941. The highlight is the giant wooden truss bridge. The trail is very accessible (even to wheelchairs).

Returning to the parking lot, head across the causeway, past Two Jack Lake. At 2.4km (1½ miles) from Minnewanka, turn left to:

❺ **Johnson Lake.** Not to be confused with Johnston Canyon, which is farther west, this man-made lake is the best place in Banff for a swim on a hot day. A flat 3.5km (2.1-mile) trail circles the lake; walk counterclockwise to take in views of Cascade Mountain.

Lake Minnewanka used to be known as "The Lake of the Water Spirits."

Bow Valley Parkway

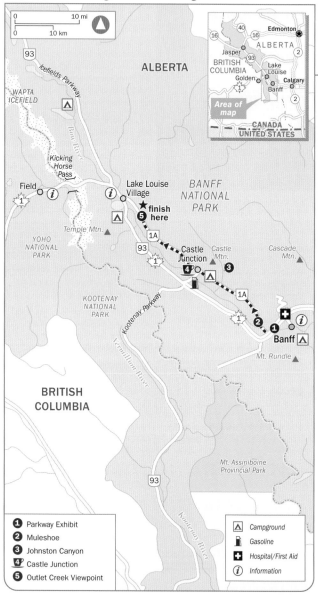

1 Parkway Exhibit
2 Muleshoe
3 Johnston Canyon
4 Castle Junction
5 Outlet Creek Viewpoint

△ Campground
🛢 Gasoline
➕ Hospital/First Aid
ⓘ Information

The Bow Valley Parkway ("Hwy. 1A") is less congested than the Trans-Canada Hwy. 1, although the two roads run parallel along the Bow River. Built in 1920—the first road connecting Banff and Lake Louise—this 51km (32-mile) route still feels more like a mountain road than an expressway. Each of the 13 interpretive stops along the way is worthwhile. I've selected the best of the bunch. The drive will take about 3 hours, including stops.

Head left (north) on Mt. Norquay Road out of the townsite and turn left (west) onto the Trans-Canada Highway. You'll meet up with the Bow Valley Parkway about 5km (3 miles) from town.

❶ Parkway Exhibit. Westbound travelers can make a quick stop at this turnoff to orient themselves to the route ahead. There is a good map and a refresher on the etiquette of wildlife encounters. *.9km (½ mile) from start of Bow Valley Pkwy.*

❷ ★ Muleshoe. A short 1km (.6 mile) trail starts across the highway from the picnic area and

The 98-foot high upper falls of Johnston Canyon.

explores the remnants of the 1993 prescribed fire. *5.5km (3½ miles) from start of Bow Valley Pkwy.*

❸ ★ Johnston Canyon. A walkway leads up this canyon, past two large waterfalls carved through limestone bedrock. The first part of the trail is on a paved surface and is a very gentle climb that ends at the first waterfall, called the Lower Falls. There are interpretive signs on the way up to the Upper Falls, almost twice the height of the Lower Falls and a further 1.6km (1 mile). *18km (11 miles) west of Banff Townsite.*

❹ Castle Junction. Three important roads meet here—the Bow Valley Parkway, Hwy. 93, and the Trans-Canada Hwy. 1. There's a gas station, a small convenience store, and cozy cabins. If you haven't already done so in the Banff Townsite, this is a good place to pick up basic picnic supplies. *28km (17 miles) from the Town of Banff.* ☎ *403/522-2783. $.*

❺ Outlet Creek Viewpoint. Here you'll find a grand view of towering Mt. Temple, the third highest peak in Banff National Park. Known as Morant's Curve, the S-bend in the Canadian Pacific Railway tracks below here offers a classic photo when eastbound trains motor through the valley. *46km (29 miles) from the start of the Bow Valley Pkwy.*

Lake Louise

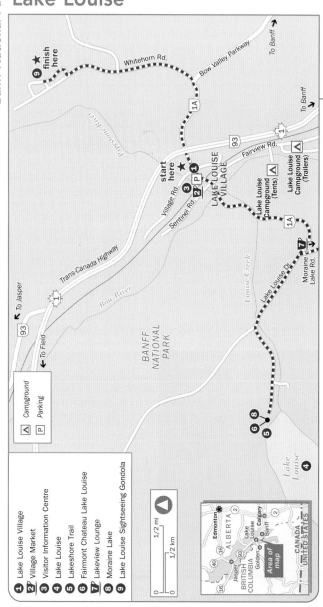

1. Lake Louise Village
2. Village Market
3. Visitor Information Centre
4. Lake Louise
5. Lakeshore Trail
6. Fairmont Chateau Lake Louise
7. Lakeview Lounge
8. Moraine Lake
9. Lake Louise Sightseeing Gondola

Campground

Parking

1/2 mi

1/2 km

start here

finish here

Whitehorn Rd.

Bow Valley Parkway

To Banff

To Banff

To Banff

Fairview Rd.

LAKE LOUISE VILLAGE

Village Rd.

Sentinel Rd.

Trans-Canada Highway

Pipestone River

Bow River

To Jasper

To Field

BANFF NATIONAL PARK

Louise Creek

Lake Louise Dr.

Moraine Lake Rd.

Lake Louise Campground (Tents)

Lake Louise Campground (Trailers)

Lake Louise

CANADA

UNITED STATES

Edmonton

ALBERTA

Lake Louise

Banff

Calgary

Golden

Jasper

BRITISH COLUMBIA

Area of map

You can't come to Banff and not see placid, beautiful Lake Louise. Situated 56km (35 miles) northwest of the Town of Banff, Lake Louise is perhaps the most photographed lake in the country, one that people from all over the world associate with their image of Canada. It's also the name of the small village just below the lake. While many people drive out just to snap a photo and then return to their hotel, it deserves a full day, with at least a short hike and time for tea.

Travel Tip

Leave your car at the village parking lot and board the shuttle up to Lake Louise if you want to avoid parking headaches at the always-packed lakeside lot. The shuttle, however, won't take you to Moraine Lake.

1 Lake Louise Village. Consisting of the key elements of a small village (or "hamlet," as Parks Canada refers to it), here you'll find gas stations, a grocery and liquor store, post office, some apartments, an ATM, restaurants, a book shop, and an outdoor equipment store. And let's not forget some outstanding hotels—which, admittedly, you might not expect to find in a small village or "hamlet." *See p 78 for Lake Louise hotels.*

2 Village Market. Amidst the trail maps and souvenirs, pop into this grocery store for picnic supplies. Although not as well stocked as the grocery stores in Banff, you can get some dips, veggies, simple sandwiches, snacks, and drinks to fill your backpack. *101 Lake Louise Dr.* ☎ *403/522-3894. $.*

3 ★ Visitor Information Centre. Housed behind Samson Mall, Parks Canada's main outpost in Lake Louise has a ton of information, including exhibits and a theater presenting the geological history of the Canadian Rockies. You can also pick up permits and maps, as well as trail, weather, and road reports. *101 Lake Louise Dr.* ☎ *403/522-3833. May 1 to mid-June 9am–5pm, mid-June to Sept 1 9am–7pm, Sept 2*

Inside a Samson Mall shop in Lake Louise Village.

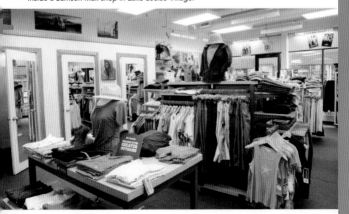

The History of the Chateau

The Chateau Lake Louise had humble beginnings, in the form of a cabin built on the site in 1890 by the CPR (Canadian Pacific Railway). By 1917 the cabin had burned to the ground, and a hotel with all the modern amenities of the day was erected in its place. While the Banff Springs Hotel, also run by the CPR, was to be luxurious, the CPR marketed the Chateau Lake Louise as a destination for outdoor adventurers. Mountaineers, artists, and horseback riders flooded in, giving the Chateau a level of popularity and character that the Springs is still striving for. With a feel akin to the Swiss Alps, mountain culture is alive and well here.

to mid-Oct 9am–5pm, mid-Oct to Apr 30 Thurs–Sun only 9am–4:30pm.

Follow Lake Louise Drive through the four-way stop, pass beneath the railway overpass, and continue. It's about 8km (5 miles) or a 5-minute drive from the village up to the lake itself and the often-crowded parking lot.

❹ ★★★ **Lake Louise.** In summer, thousands of people empty out of bus tours in front of the lake each day to have their picture taken, then jump back on to the bus and head off to the next tour stop. It's quite crowded. But the lake is so beautiful and pristine, you should go anyway. Fed by glacial meltwater, Lake Louise is 2.4km (1½ miles) long, 500m (1,640 ft.) wide, and 90m (295 ft.) deep. Behind it is **Mt. Victoria,** at an elevation of 3,464m (11,365 ft.), with the thick **Victoria Glacier** on its front ridge. The lake was named after Princess Louise Caroline Alberta (1849–1939), the fourth daughter of Queen Victoria and later the wife of the governor-general of Canada.

❺ ★ **Lakeshore Trail.** This is a 2km (1.2-mile) path (each way) that runs from the Chateau along the

Marvelous views accompany the meals at Fairmont Chateau Lake Louise.

A hiker takes a break overlooking Moraine Lake.

lake's north shore to the western end of the lake. At the back of the lake, quartzite crags are popular with rock climbers. It's open to walkers May through October, depending on snow, and to skiers the rest of the year.

6 ★ Fairmont Chateau Lake Louise. Often called a "diamond in the wilderness," this is an impressive and important hotel rich in history and obviously blessed with an incredible setting. If you aren't a guest, you are welcome to come in for a meal, some shopping or tea, or just to roam and wonder at the fantastic ambience. *See p 79.*

7 It's all quite civilized inside the **Lakeview Lounge,** a superb place for an afternoon tea at the Chateau Lake Louise. The view, stretching across the lake, is divine. Traditional afternoon tea service includes sandwiches, scones, sweets, and polished silver. ☎ *403/522-1818. www.fairmont.com/lake-louise Tea served daily noon–4pm. $$$.*

There is a winding road (open only May through October) that takes you the 13km (8 miles) from Lake Louise to Moraine Lake. At the often-crowded parking lot are a lodge, a picnic area, and some interpretive exhibits.

9 ★★★ Moraine Lake. Just south of Lake Louise is another stunning alpine lake, situated in front of the Valley of the Ten Peaks. Wild and dramatic, Moraine Lake is very popular. You can rent canoes here for $39 per hour, or walk an excellent interpretive trail to the Moraine Lake Rockpile for the view that used to be on the Canadian $20 bill. Moraine Lake is also the trail head for a number of the best hikes in Banff National Park (see chapter 6).

Head back to the Lake Louise Road, down to the village, over the Trans-Canada Hwy. 1 and up Whitehorn Road to:

10 ★★ kids Lake Louise Sightseeing Gondola. In the summer, take a gondola to the summit of Whitehorn Mountain for excellent views of the Bow Valley, Lake Louise, and the Continental Divide. Naturalists lead guided hikes that are great interactive learning experiences. Grizzly bears have been known to hang out here in the summer, so going with a guide is a wise idea. *At the top of Whitehorn Rd.* ☎ *403/522-3555. www.lakelouise gondola.com. Adults $32, child 6–15 $16, kids 5 and under free. May 13–June 19 9am–4pm, June 20–Aug 1 8:30am–5:30pm, Aug 2–Sept 5 8:30am–6pm, Sept 6–Oct 9 10am–4pm.*

The Icefields Parkway

ALBERTA

BRITISH COLUMBIA

BANFF NATIONAL PARK

WAPTA ICEFIELD

FRESHFIELD ICEFIELD

LYELL ICEFIELD

Siffleur Wilderness

YOHO NATIONAL PARK

KOOTENAY NATIONAL PARK

Park Gate

Saskatchewan Crossing

Park Gate

Kicking Horse Pass

Field

Lake Louise Village

Temple Mtn.

Saskatchewan River

Bow River

Icefields Parkway

93

start here

finish here

Inset map:
Edmonton
ALBERTA
Jasper
BRITISH COLUMBIA
Golden
Lake Louise
Banff
Calgary
Area of map
CANADA
UNITED STATES

Legend:
- △ Campground
- 🛢 Gasoline
- ✚ Hospital/First Aid
- ⓘ Information
- ▢ Point of Interest

1 Crowfoot Glacier
2 Bow Lake
3a Bow Summit
3b Peyto Lake
4 Waterfowl Lake
5 Mistaya Canyon
6 Saskatchewan Crossing
7 Weeping Wall
8 Big Bend and Big Hill
9a Sunwapta Pass
9b Jasper National Park border
10 Athabasca Glacier

0   10 mi
0   10 km

The landscape you see on the spectacular Icefields Parkway is the kind that used to dominate western North America. Hwy. 93, the Icefields Parkway, connects Banff and Jasper national parks, and along the way you'll be wowed by raging rivers, turquoise lakes, glacier-clad summits, and massive icefields. The hiking trails and the wildlife viewing are outstanding. Plan to get out of your car often! This tour only covers the highway as far as the Icefields Centre. For information on continuing on to Jasper, see p 98.

Travel Tip

If you haven't already got one, pick up a detailed map and guide to the Icefields Parkway from the Lake Louise Visitors Centre, in Lake Louise's Samson Mall (101 Lake Louise Dr.; ☎ 403/522-3833).

Continuing north on the Icefields Parkway, the road steadily climbs higher and higher and the views become more and more dramatic as you make your way through three river valleys and pass beneath towering glacier-topped peaks.

❶ **Crowfoot Glacier.** It's the first of a long lineup of glaciers you'll see. There are interpretive signs posted at the roadside viewpoint. It's a good spot to contemplate the shrinking of the world's glaciers and the impact of climate change. *33km*

(21 miles) north of the Trans-Canada Hwy. 1 junction at Lake Louise.

❷ ★ **Bow Lake.** This ice-blue lake is the third-largest in Banff National Park. Almost all of its water is glacier-fed; you can just see the Bow Glacier at the back of the lake. It's a nice place for a picnic. The red-roofed inn on the lake's northeast shore is Num-Ti-Jah Lodge (p 81). *34km (21 miles) north of the Trans-Canada Hwy. 1 junction at Lake Louise.*

❸ ★★ **Bow Summit and Peyto Lake.** At an elevation of 2,069m (6,788 ft.), you're at the highest point in Canada that can be crossed by a highway year-round. Walk the short interpretive trail at Bow Summit to see this beautiful turquoise lake set far below the lookout in a deep glacial valley. It's named for pioneer guide "Wild"

Sunrise at Crowfoot Mountain and Crowfoot Glacier.

Bow Lake, the third-largest in Banff National Park.

Bill Peyto, who was a warden in Banff National Park. Continue further along a short extension of the trail, going left and up the hill, for views of the glacier that feeds the lake. *40km (25 miles) north of the Trans-Canada Hwy. 1 junction at Lake Louise.*

Heading north past Peyto Lake, the landscape becomes more barren and beautiful.

❹ **Waterfowl Lake.** Stop at the pullout next to this serene lake to view some of the mighty peaks along the Continental Divide. In fact, all of the mountains on the

The Mistaya River descends through Mistaya Canyon.

west side of the Icefields Parkway form part of the backbone of the continent. From here, you can see Howse Peak and Mt. Chephren, a classically horned peak resembling a pyramid. *56km (35 miles) north of the Trans-Canada Hwy. 1 junction at Lake Louise.*

❺ ★ **Mistaya Canyon.** Deep and steep, the beauty of this canyon is in its sublimely curvy walls, the fierce roar of the water, and in the quiet trail, much quieter than at the other famous canyons in the Rockies. The Mistaya River drops off Bow Summit and has carved out a series of potholes along the canyon's walls. A steep but short .5km (.3 mile) trail leads from the north end of a parking lot on the west side of the Icefields Parkway down into to the canyon. *71km (44 miles) north of the Trans-Canada Hwy. 1 junction at Lake Louise.*

❻ **Saskatchewan Crossing.** On the banks of the Saskatchewan River, there is a warden station, gas station, snack bar, and gift shop at a basic roadside complex called "The Crossing." It's a good place to get out and stretch your legs. *77km (48 miles) north of the Trans-Canada Hwy. 1 junction with the start of the Icefields Pkwy. 93.*

Pull over on the west side of the highway to get a look at:

❼ The Weeping Wall. In summer you may see only a few drops of water wetting the ridge on the east side of the highway, but in the winter these drips and drops freeze to create a huge frozen waterfall draped in layer upon layer of ice. This is a hot spot for the technical sport of ice climbing. *106km (66 miles) north of the Trans-Canada Hwy. 1 junction at Lake Louise.*

❽ Big Bend and Big Hill. A famous hairpin turn is followed by a steep hill, both of which are excruciatingly difficult for cyclists. There is a pullout at the top of the hill with a nice view of Bridal View Falls. *111km (69 miles) north of the Trans-Canada Hwy. 1 junction at Lake Louise.*

❾ Sunwapta Pass and Jasper National Park. At 2,023m (6,637 ft.), this is the second highest point on the Icefields Parkway and forms the border between Banff and Jasper national parks. It's also the border between the two watersheds: The North Saskatchewan River drains from here to Lake Winnipeg, Hudson Bay, and the Atlantic Ocean, while on the other side of the pass the Sunwapta River eventually makes its way to the Arctic Ocean. It's all downhill from here—108km (67 miles) north on the Icefields Parkway to Jasper Townsite.

Water flows down the Weeping Wall in warm weather, but freezes beautifully in winter, making it a favorite ice-climbing spot.

122km (76 miles) north of the Trans-Canada Hwy. 1 junction at Lake Louise.

❿ ★★ Athabasca Glacier. With its tongue almost touching the highway, this is the most accessible of the six principal glaciers that make up the Columbia Icefield, and is also the most visited glacier in North America. It's receding 2 to 3m (6½– 9¾ ft.) each year. Park your car at the Toe-of-the-Glacier trail head (which was covered by ice in the 1950s) and walk down through lunar-like landscape to the ice. Don't venture onto the ice without a guide (see below). For information on the Athabasca glacier tours, see p 17. *127km (79 miles) north of the Trans-Canada Hwy. 1 junction at Lake Louise.*

Icewalk Interpretive Tours

More adventurous folk will prefer to join a certified mountain guide who leaves daily from the Toe-of-the-Glacier parking lot for guided hikes that allow you to walk on the ice. Hikes for 3 to 4 hours cost $95 for adults and $50 for kids 7 to 16 (kids 6 and under not allowed). More strenuous—and more exploratory—6-hour hikes cost $120 for adults, $60 for kids 7 to 16. Call ☎ 800/565-7547 or see www.icewalks.com.

Dining in **Banff National Park**

1888 Chop House **22**
The Balkan **20**
Baker Creek Bistro **1**
Barpa Bill's **10**
Bear Street Tavern **12**
The Bison **12**
Bow Valley Grill **22**
Chaya **20**
Coyotes Grill **16**

Eddie Burger + Bar **17**
Elk & Oarsmen **19**
Evelyn's **14**
Grizzly House **15**
JK Bakery **9**
Juniper Bistro **2**
The Keg at Caribou Lodge **5**
Maple Leaf Grill **18**
Nourish **12**

Old Spaghetti Factory **8**
The Outpost **4**
Park Distillery **14**
Post Hotel **3**
Saltlik **11**
Sleeping Buffalo **6**
Three Ravens **21**
Whitebark Café **7**
Wild Flour **13**

Dining Best Bets

Best for Adventurous Kids
Grizzly House $$ 207 Banff Ave. (p 72)

Best Bakery
Wild Flour Bakery $ 211 Bear St.
(p 75)

Best Breakfast
★★ Coyotes Grill $$
206 Caribou St. (p 71)

Best Brunch
★★ Bow Valley Grill $$ In the
Fairmont Banff Springs Hotel.
405 Spray Ave. (p 71)

Best Burger
★ Eddie Burger + Bar $
137C Banff Ave. (p 71)

Best Canadiana Cool
★★ Maple Leaf Grill $$
137 Banff Ave. (p 73)

Best Cheap Bowl of Hot Soup
Chaya $ 118 Banff Ave. (p 71)

Best Coffee
★★ Whitebark Café $
401 Banff Ave. (p 75)

Best for Eating Family-Style
★ Park Distillery $$ 219 Banff Ave.
(p 74)

Best for Health Freaks
Nourish $$ 215 Banff Ave., second
floor (p 73)

Best for Locavores
★★ The Bison $$$ 211 Bear St.
(p 71)

Best Mediterranean
The Balkan $$ 120 Banff Ave. (p. 70)

**Best for Parents with No
Babysitter**
Old Spaghetti Factory $ Cascade
Plaza, 317 Banff Ave., second floor
(p 73)

Best Patio
Juniper Bistro $ In the Juniper Hotel,
bottom of Mt. Norquay Rd. (p 73)

Best Pizza
★★ Bear Street Tavern $$
211 Bear St. (p 70)

Best Pub Food
★ Elk & Oarsmen $$ Upstairs,
119 Banff Ave. (p 72)

Best Sandwiches-to-Go
JK Bakery $ 229 Bear St. (p 73)

Best Splurge
★★ 1888 Chop House $$$ In the
Fairmont Banff Springs Hotel,
Spray Ave. (p 70)

Best Steakhouse
★★ Saltlik $$ In the Fairmont Banff
Springs Hotel, 405 Spray Ave. (p 74)

Best Takeout
Barpa Bill's $ 233 Bear St. (p 70)

Best View
Three Ravens $$ At The Banff
Centre, St. Julien Rd. (p 75)

Best Wine Cellar
★★★ Post Hotel $$$
200 Pipestone Rd. (p 74)

**Best Place Worth the Drive
from Banff**
★ Baker Creek Bistro $$ 11km
(6¾ miles) southeast of Lake Louise
and 14 km (8¾ miles) north of Castle
Junction on the Bow Valley Pkwy.,
Hwy. 1A. (p 70)

Seafood from Maple Leaf Grille.

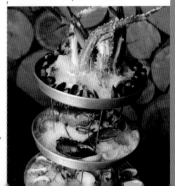

Restaurants A to Z

★★ 1888 Chop House BANFF *STEAKHOUSE* The newest restaurant at the Fairmont Banff Springs Hotel is definitely worth a visit. The menu is focused straight on high-end cuts of Alberta beef. Order a dry-aged rib-eye or porterhouse, with thyme-roasted yams and maple carrots on the side. It's decadent and all very delicious. Everything, from the butter to the cocktail garnishes, is made in house. *In the Fairmont Banff Springs Hotel, 405 Spray Ave.* ☎ *403/762-6860. www.fairmont.com/banff. Entrees $38–$62. AE, DC, MC, V. Tues–Sat 6pm–9pm. Map p 68.*

kids The Balkan BANFF *GREEK* The recipes at this family-owned Banff landmark come from the old country—souvlaki, moussaka, arni psito, and donair pitas (great for lunch). This is a great place for sharing. A new decor oozes Mediterranean sunshine. On Tuesdays and most Thursdays, the place comes alive with belly-dancing and plate-smashing. *120 Banff Ave.* ☎ *403/762-3454. www.banffbalkan.ca. Entrees $14–$29. AE, MC, V. Daily 11am–11pm. Map p 68.*

★ Baker Creek Bistro LAKE LOUISE *REGIONAL* Fresh and modern food is served by warm and friendly folks inside a heritage cabin just south of Lake Louise. It makes a great pit stop on your way to Lake Louise or the Icefields Parkway. *11km (6¾ miles) southeast of Lake Louise and 14km (8¾ miles) north of Castle Junction on the Bow Valley Pkwy., Hwy. 1A.* ☎ *403/522-2182. www.bakercreekbistro.com. Entrees $18–$33. AE, MC, V. Daily noon–3pm and 5–9pm. Map p 68.*

Barpa Bill's BANFF *GREEK* For something "to go," you can't beat a souvlaki in a warm pita, hot off the grill at this little Bear Street joint. It's topped with fresh tzatziki sauce and cooked to order. There are also gyros, burgers, and poutine, a French-Canadian specialty. Grab a stool at the counter if you want to eat in, but don't expect friendly chatter with the staff! *233 Bear St.* ☎ *403/762-0377. www.barpabills. com. Entrees $9–$14. No credit cards. Daily 11am–9pm. Map p 68.*

★★ Bear Street Tavern BANFF *PIZZA* For a bite and pint with

The Bison is home to Rocky Mountain comfort food.

A hearty dish from the Fairmont Banff Springs' Bow Valley Grill.

friends after skiing or biking, this happening spot is my first choice in town. The thin-crust pizza is superbly good—try the Wheeler Hut with wild mushrooms, pine nuts, truffle oil, and pesto. They also have gluten-free pizza. For something hearty, try the pork belly macaroni and cheese. There are local beers on tap and daily cocktail specials. *211 Bear St., main floor.* ☎ *403/762-2021. www.bearstreet tavern.ca. Entrees $13–$19. AE, MC, V. Daily 11:30am–midnight. Map p 68.*

★★ **The Bison** BANFF *REGIONAL* Regional and seasonal "Rocky Mountain comfort food" is perfectly suited for Banff. The classic dish is grilled bison rib steak. Or try daily game. Everything except the pickles and mayonnaise is made from scratch. The outdoor patio is the nicest in town. *211 Bear St., upstairs.* ☎ *403/762-5550. www.thebison.ca. Entrees $16–$45. AE, MC, V. Mon–Fri 11am–10:30pm, Sat–Sun 10am–10:30pm. Map p 68.*

★★ **Bow Valley Grill** BANFF *CANADIAN* With an open concept kitchen and a gorgeous setting inside the Fairmont Banff Springs, this is the best brunch in town. Summertime brings market-style buffets. In wintertime, it's à la carte. *In the Fairmont Banff Springs*

Hotel, 405 Spray Ave. ☎ *403/762-6860. www.fairmont.com/banff springs. Entrees $28–$42. AE, DC, MC, V. Daily 7am–11pm, 6–9pm; Sat brunch 11:30am–1:30pm, Sun brunch 11am–2pm. Map p 68.*

Chaya BANFF *ASIAN* After a few hours in the fresh air, the big bowls of steaming Asian soups at Chaya hit the spot. This small spot next to McDonald's is as popular with Banff's quite large Japanese-Canadian population as it is with tourists. Try the Udon noodles or teriyaki rice bowls. The miso ramen bowl comes with ground pork and has a nice spicy kick. It's very small inside, and it can be tough to get a table in peak hours. *118 Banff Ave.* ☎ *403/760-0882. Entrees $10–$14. Daily 11:30am–8pm. Map p 68.*

★★ **Coyotes Grill** BANFF *SOUTHWESTERN* Fresh, healthy, relaxed, and very popular with locals, Santa Fe comes to the Rockies here with corn and chile peppers on enchiladas, in soups, and even on pizzas. There's also a superb breakfast. *206 Caribou St.* ☎ *403/762-3963. www.coyotes banff.com. Entrees $17–$29. AE, MC, V. Daily 7:30am–11pm. Map p 68.*

★ **Eddie Burger + Bar** BANFF *BURGERS* Build your own gourmet burgers well into the evening at this fun and funky bar. The bison burger comes with sautéed mushrooms,

Diners at Bear Street Tavern.

Evelyn's is a favorite for coffee or lunch.

double-smoked bacon, and roasted garlic aioli on an English muffin. Add sweet potato fries and a milkshake. *137C Banff Ave. (on Caribou St.).* ☎ *403/762-2230. www.eddie burgerbar.ca. Entrees $8–$16. MC, V. Daily 11:30am–3am. Map p 68.*

★ **Elk & Oarsmen** BANFF *PUB* Settle in with some locals to watch the game and dig into the best pub food in Banff. Recommended choices are the Black Angus steaks or a burger (you have elk, bison, beef, salmon, or chorizo to choose from!). There's a great patio on the rooftop, regular happy-hour specials, and big screen TVs. *119 Banff Ave., second floor.* ☎ *403/762-4616. www.elkandoarsman.com. Entrees $14–$32. AE, MC, V. Daily 11am–11pm (pub stays open later). Map p 68.*

Evelyn's BANFF *COFFEESHOP* There are two Evelyn's along Banff Avenue, both popular for coffees,

pies, big and hearty sandwiches, and giant-sized gourmet cookies, which make for great picnics or hiking treats. There aren't many seats here; this is a place to grab something and take it with you skiing, hiking or over to the benches along the Bow River. *215 Banff Ave.* ☎ *403/762-0352. www.evelyns coffeebar.com. Entrees $8–$12. MC, V. Daily 7am–6pm. Map p 68.*

Grizzly House BANFF *FONDUE* Fondue has never gone out of style at this over-the-top alcove on Banff Avenue. Veggie, chicken, prawn, beef, even buffalo can get dropped into the pot. There's plenty of retroshtick here to temper the steaming pots of fondue and the smoking hot plates. Things can get rowdy and noisy in here, though. *207 Banff Ave.* ☎ *403/762-4055. www.banff grizzlyhouse.com. Entrees $17–$48. AE, MC, V. Daily 11:30am–midnight. Map p 68.*

A meal with view at Juniper Bistro.

JK Bakery BANFF *DELI* Build your own sandwiches to take for a picnic at this busy little cafe beneath the local movie theatre. There are also well-priced daily lunch specials like lasagna and chili, and superb baked goods. *229 Bear St.* ☎ *403/760-0800. Lunch $7–$11. AE, MC, V. Mon–Sat 8:30am–5pm. Map p 68.*

Juniper Bistro BANFF *CANADIAN* Just out of town, the main draw to this bistro is its sunny patio, one of the nicest in town. The menu has hearty pub food, like dark ale bison ribs and a fish hot pot. *Bottom of Mt. Norquay Rd. in the Juniper Hotel.* ☎ *403/763-6205. www.thejuniper.com. Entrees $18–$34. AE, MC, V. Daily 7:30am–9:30pm. Map p 68.*

The Keg at Caribou Lodge BANFF *STEAKHOUSE* They've got everything from filet mignons to rib steaks, but the stars here are grilled sirloins and prime rib. There are two Keg locations in Banff, both along Banff Avenue. But the one inside the Caribou Lodge has a cozy, wooden-framed atmosphere, great service and consistently top-notch steaks. They are also open for breakfast. *521 Banff Ave.* ☎ *403/762-4442. www.kegsteakhouse.com. Entrees $21–$38. AE, MC, V. Daily 6:30am–midnight. Map p 68.*

★★ Maple Leaf Grill BANFF *CANADIAN* Canadian classics like rainbow trout and venison vie with Alberta bison and Atlantic salmon beneath a birchbark canoe in a room that feels more like a lodge. Although casual in atmosphere, the food is decidedly upscale. There's an award-winning wine list with over 100 Canadian labels. *137 Banff Ave.* ☎ *403/760-7680. www.banffmapleleaf.com. Entrees $22–$48. AE, MC, V. Daily 10am–2am. Map p 68.*

Nourish BANFF *VEGETARIAN* If you're tired of steaks and gamey meat, this friendly second-floor restaurant in the Sundance Mall has organic, vegan, wheat-free, and gluten-free choices. Even non-vegetarians will like the nacho platter or wild-mushroom ravioli with lavender sauce. The decor is funky and colorful. *215 Banff Ave.* ☎ *403/760-3933. www.nourishbistro.com. Entrees $16–$27. AE, MC, V. Wed–Mon noon–3pm, 5–9pm. Map p 68.*

kids Old Spaghetti Factory BANFF *ITALIAN* Expect no-frills Italian specialties like lasagna and pesto linguini. Entrees all include soup or salad, garlic bread, and an ice cream dessert. There are always great specials and bargains here, especially for families. *Cascade*

Nourish has excellent vegetarian options.

Trendy Saltlik is known for its steaks.

Plaza, 317 Banff Ave., second floor. ☎ 403/760-2779. www.oldspaghetti factory.ca. Entrees $10–$16. AE, MC, V. Daily 11:30am–10pm. Map p 68.

★ **The Outpost** LAKE LOUISE *PUB* This English-style pub happens to be joined to one of the finest dining establishments in Canada, the Post Hotel. So you can expect no-fuss (burgers, pizzas, quesadillas, and so on) with exquisite standards. I recommend the veal bratwurst with rosti potatoes and onion sauce. 200 Pipestone Rd. ☎ 403/522-3989. www.posthotel. com. Entrees $16–$25. AE, MC, V. Mon–Fri 4:30pm–midnight, Sat–Sun noon–midnight. Map p 68.

★ **Park Distillery** BANFF REGIONAL The newest eatery in town is fun. Eat family-style meals inspired by a campfire like barbecue ribs, pork 'n' beans, and coleslaw. And don't miss the cornbread with maple butter. You can also sample their in-house vodkas, ryes, and whiskeys. There are plenty of good options for kids. 219 Banff Ave.

☎ 403/762-5114. www.parkdistillery. com. Entrees $15–$46. AE, MC, V. Daily 11am–midnight. Map p 68.

★★★ **Post Hotel** LAKE LOUISE *REGIONAL* Blending fine dining with a rustic elegance, the Swiss chef uses European techniques and regional ingredients, mainly meats like veal tenderloin, caribou strip-loin, and rack of lamb. Service is first-class. The real star, though, is a massive wine cellar. 200 Pipestone Rd. ☎ 403/522-2167. www.post hotel.com. Entrees $32–$52. AE, MC, V. Daily 11:30am–2pm, 6–10pm. Map p 68.

★★ **Saltlik** BANFF *STEAKHOUSE* With a modern, trendy twist, steaks here are fast-cooked in a 1,200°F (649°C) infrared oven. Top it with a marinade like chipotle barbecue or citrus rosemary. A lounge downstairs features live jazz and martinis. 221 Bear St. ☎ 403/762-2467. www. saltlik.com. Entrees $19–$44. AE, MC, V. Daily noon–1am. Map p 68.

★ **Sleeping Buffalo** BANFF *REGIONAL* One of the earliest promoters of Rocky Mountain cuisine, there is an impressive selection of very local meats here. The sample platter has smoked buffalo, venison ham, and elk salami. An incredibly tender bison rib-eye stands out in the entrees list. *700 Tunnel Mountain Rd. at the Buffalo Mountain Lodge.* 📞 *403/ 760-4484. www.crmr.com/buffalo/ dining. Entrees $26–$38. Daily noon– 10pm. Map p 68.*

Three Ravens Restaurant and Wine Bar BANFF REGIONAL

Hands down the place to eat with the best view in Banff is up here at the top of the impressive Banff Centre. The menu is high-end, intricate and features quality ingredients from across western Canada. There's a slightly less expensive buffet-style option right next door. Or just come for a drink and tapas at the wine bar before taking in a show. *Top floor, Sally Borden Building, 107 Tunnel Mountain Dr.* 📞 *403/762- 6300. www.banffcentre.ca/dining. Entrees $30–$41. AE, MC, V. Daily 5–9pm, wine bar daily 4pm–midnight. Map p 68.*

★★ Whitebark Café BANFF

CAFE Finally a first-rate espresso bar in Banff! This is the place to grab a latte, cappuccino or macchiato, catch up on the local paper, and enjoy the sunny morning patio in summer. In classic espresso bar style, it's a small spot, with only a stand-up bar inside. But the coffee is worth it. They also have a great, affordable light lunch special (usually a quiche or quinoa salad). *401 Banff Ave.* 📞 *403/762-7298. www. whitebarkcafe.com. Lunch $7–$9. MC, V. Daily 6:30am–6pm. Map p 68.*

Wild Flour Bakery and Café

BANFF CAFE Bustling from dawn to dusk, this is Banff's best bakery and a great spot for lunch. Their sandwiches are excellent—try the pulled pork with apple barbecue sauce or the gourmet grilled cheese. There's always a soup and focaccia of the day. Grab a protein bar for an afternoon snack. *221 Bear St.* 📞 *403/760-5074. www.wildflour bakery.ca. Entrees $7–$10. AE, MC, V. Mon–Thurs 7am–6pm, Fri–Sat 7am–6pm. Map p 68.*

Dine with a view at Three Ravens Restaurant.

Lodging in Banff National Park

Baker Creek Chalets 21
Banff Alpine Centre 3
Banff Aspen Lodge 10
A Banff Boutique Inn –
  Pension Tannenhof 11
Buffalo Mountain Lodge 5
Buffaloberry Bed & Breakfast 8
Fairmont Banff Springs Hotel 13
Fairmont Chateau Lake Louise 18
Fox Hotel and Suites 7

Hidden Ridge Resort 4
Johnston Canyon Campground 9
Lake Louise Alpine Centre 17
Lake Louise Campground 20
Num-Ti-Jah Lodge 14
Post Hotel 19
Rimrock Resort Hotel 12
Rundlestone Lodge 6
Skoki Lodge 16
Storm Mountain Lodge 23
Sunshine Mountain Lodge 22
Tunnel Mountain Village Campground 2
Two Jack Campground 1
Waterfowl Lake Campground 15

Lodging Best Bets

Best **Backcountry**
★★ Skoki Lodge $$ *In Banff National Park; access from trail head at Temple Lodge next to Lake Louise Ski Resort (p 82)*

Best **Boutique Hotel**
★ A Banff Boutique Inn—Pension Tannenhof $$ *121 Cave Ave. (p 78)*

Best **on a Budget**
Banff Aspen Lodge $ *401 Banff Ave. (p 78)*

Best **for Business**
Rimrock Resort Hotel $$$ *300 Mountain Ave. (p 81)*

Best **Historic Charm**
★★ Post Hotel $$$ *200 Pipestone Rd. (p 81)*

Best **for Families**
Fox Hotel and Suites $$ *46 Banff Ave. (p 79)*

Best **for Meeting Hiking Partners**
Banff Alpine Centre $ *801 Hidden Ridge Way (p 78)*

Best **Local Knowledge**
★ A Banff Boutique Inn—Pension Tannenhof $$ *121 Cave Ave. (p 78)*

Best **Night's Sleep**
Buffaloberry Bed and Breakfast $$ *417 Marten St. (p 79)*

Best **Scenery**
Num-Ti-Jah Lodge $$ *Icefields Pkwy. (p 81)*

Best **for Skiers**
Sunshine Mountain Lodge, $$ *at Sunshine Village Ski Resort (p 82)*

Best **Spa**
★★ Willow Stream at the Fairmont Banff Springs $$$ *405 Spray Ave. (p 79)*

Best **View**
★★ Fairmont Chateau Lake Louise $$$ *111 Lake Louise Dr. (p 79)*

Best **for Wildlife Watching**
★ Baker Creek Chalets $$ *11km (6¾ miles) southeast of Lake Louise and 14km (8¾ miles) north of Castle Junction on the Bow Valley Pkwy., Hwy. 1A. (p 78)*

The scenery at Num-Ti-Jah Lodge is hard to beat.

Lodging A to Z

Travel Tip

All prices given are for summer rates, which are in effect from about June 15 to September 15. If you travel outside this peak season—except for around the Christmas holidays—rates should be lower. Check the hotel's websites for packages and deals.

★ kids Baker Creek Chalets

LAKE LOUISE   In a semi-secluded spot just south of Lake Louise, this collection of red-roofed cabins and lodges is really amidst the wild—bears, elk, and deer routinely strolling by. Cabins mainly sleep four to six and have kitchenettes. It's the kind of place you want to settle in and spend an entire week, well worth at least a night or two away from busy Banff. The train runs sporadically throughout the day and night next to the property; if you are a light sleeper, ask for their quietest cabins. *11km (6¾ miles) southeast of Lake Louise and 14km (8¾ miles) north of Castle Junction on the Bow Valley Pkwy., Hwy. 1A.* ☎ *403/522-2270. www.bakercreek.com. 35 units. Doubles $285–$405. AE, MC, V. Map p 76.*

Banff Alpine Centre BANFF

Fun and reasonably priced, this hostel is just outside the Banff Townsite on Tunnel Mountain Road. Dorm rooms sleep four to six people, and there are five double rooms with private bathrooms that are a good bargain. The pub is always lively. *801 Hidden Ridge Way.* ☎ *403/762-4123. www.hihostels.ca/alberta. 52 units, which accommodate btw. 2 and 6 people, or 216 beds. Beds from $37; private doubles from $123. MC, V. Map p 76.*

Banff Aspen Lodge BANFF   An

inexpensive option in a good location, this Banff Avenue hotel has undergone a pretty chic and hip upgrade. Rooms are well-priced, all looking out on an interior patio with hot tubs. Breakfast is included. Start your day in the lobby at the town's best espresso bar. *401 Banff Ave.* ☎ *403/762-4401. www.banffaspenlodge.com. 89 rooms. Doubles from $139, breakfast included. MC, V. Map p 76.*

★ A Banff Boutique Inn—Pension Tannenhof BANFF   A

local couple with a passion for innkeeping has turned an old-fashioned building into a lovely inn, with modern decor and mountain hospitality. It's a breath of fresh air in Banff. Rooms have strange layouts, some with very small bathrooms, but the vibe is relaxing and breakfasts superb. *121 Cave Ave.*

Inside a cabin at Baker Creek Chalets.

The Fairmont Banff Springs Hotel is one of the most famous buildings in Canada.

403/762-4636. www.banffboutique inn.com. 10 units. Doubles $175–$310. Breakfast included. MC, V. Map p 76.

Buffalo Mountain Lodge

BANFF   With peeled log frames, feather duvets over flannel sheets, fieldstone fireplaces, and log furniture, there's a preppy cottage feel to this collection of buildings on Tunnel Mountain. There's a casually elegant, outdoorsy feel here. *700 Tunnel Mountain Rd.* 800/661-1367 or 403/762-2400. www.crmr. com. 108 units. Doubles $259–$349. AE, MC, V. Map p 76.

Buffaloberry Bed & Breakfast

BANFF   The unpretentious owners of this little inn love the outdoors, and their B&B, in a building nestled in one of downtown Banff's quieter areas, may be the best sleep in town, thanks to soundproof rooms, blackout curtains, solid-core doors, and luxurious natural linens. Bathrooms are spacious. *417 Marten St.* 403/762-3750. www.buffaloberry. com. 4 units. Doubles $335. Breakfast included. MC, V. Map p 76.

★★ Fairmont Banff Springs

Hotel BANFF   One of the most famous buildings in Canada, this spectacular hotel is a true experience. Rooms are notoriously small, so don't plan to spend much time indoors. The Gold Floor has by far the nicest rooms. The list of amenities, from the Willow Stream Spa,

to a bowling center, horse stables, and nine restaurants, overwhelms. This is an unforgettable place to spend a few nights, but it doesn't come cheap. Packages including breakfasts and online specials will help with the high price tag. *405 Spray Ave.* 800/441-1414 or 403/762-2211. www.fairmont.com/ banffsprings. 768 units. Doubles $449–659. AE, DC, MC, V. Map p 76.

★★ Fairmont Chateau Lake

Louise LAKE LOUISE   The award-winning landmark hotel is elegant, with a Swiss Alpine feel, and more comfortable than the Banff Springs. Rooms with lake views are much more than those on the other side of the hall (which still have nice mountain views). The Gold Floor offers superior service. All the rooms and public spaces have been recently updated. The pool is nothing special, but the hotel's rich heritage, coupled with access to amazing hiking and skiing, is unmatched on the planet. *111 Lake Louise Dr.* 800/441-1414 or 403/522-3511. www.fairmont.com/ lakelouise. 554 units. Doubles $349–$499. AE, DC, MC, V. Map p 76.

kids Fox Hotel and Suites

BANFF   More contemporary than most of the hotels in town, rooms are mostly suites with kitchenettes and one or two bedrooms. Loft-style second-floor units have mountain views. The courtyard has a

A room with a view of the lake at Fairmont Chateau Lake Louise.

stunning hot pool themed after the historic Banff springs. *46 Banff Ave.* ☎ *800/661-8310 or 403/760-8500. www.bestofbanff.com/fox. 117 units. Doubles $219–$449. AE, MC, V. Map p 76.*

Hidden Ridge Resort BANFF If you'd like lots of personal space, and to be away from the bustle of Banff Avenue, this collection of stylish cabins along Tunnel Mountain Road provides privacy in townhouse–style apartments. All units have full kitchens and wood-burning fireplaces. Two outdoor hot pools offer fabulous views overlooking Banff. *901 Hidden Ridge Way.* ☎ *800/661-1372 or 403/762-3544. www.bestof banff.com/hrr. 107 units. Chalets $199–$469. AE, MC, V. Map p 76.*

Johnston Canyon Campground This is a tranquil campground nestled in a pleasant forest less than 20 minutes from Banff Townsite. The nicest of the sites back onto Johnston Creek. *25km (16 miles) west of Banff Townsite on the Bow Valley*

Pkwy., Hwy. 1A. No reservations. 132 sites. No RV hookups. Sites $27. AE, MC, V. Closed Sept 15–May 28. Map p 76.

Lake Louise Alpine Centre LAKE LOUISE Don't let the fact that this is a hostel turn you off a great value. Rooms range from small dormitories and simple doubles to larger rooms that sleep up to six. Simple communal bathrooms and showers are down the hall. *203 Village Rd.* ☎ *403/522-2201. www. hostellingintl.ca/alberta. 45 units. Dorms from $38. Private rooms from $120. MC, V. Map p 76.*

Lake Louise Campground LAKE LOUISE This campground is downhill from the Fairmont Chateau Lake Louise, away from the lake. The tent area is in the trees near the river. The trailer area is more open and closer to the highway and railway line. It's a 10-minute walk to Lake Louise Village. *58km (36 miles) northwest of Banff Townsite on the Trans-Canada*

A bedroom inside the Fox Hotel and Suites.

Hwy. 1. Exit at Lake Louise and turn left after passing under the railway bridge onto Fairview Rd. Reservations at www.pccamping.ca. ☎ *877/737-3783. Lake Louise Tent: 206 sites. No RV hookups. $28. Closed Sept 30–May 25. Lake Louise Trailer: 189 sites. Electrical hookups only. $32. Open year-round. Map p 76.*

Num-Ti-Jah Lodge ICEFIELDS PARKWAY Banff's most scenic lodge is rustic, historic, and secluded. You'll pay for the location, and the expensive dining room (which is the only option), not the amenities. The stairs creak as you climb them and the walls are thin. Rooms are clean, though quite basic. Heaps of character and history manage to cover up the need for a major upgrade. *40km (25 miles) north of Lake Louise on the Icefields Pkwy.* ☎ *403/522-2167. www.num-ti-jah.com. 25 units. Doubles $275–$320. AE, MC, V. Map p 76.*

★★ Post Hotel LAKE LOUISE A quintessential and exquisite mountain inn, the Post Hotel combines beautiful guest rooms and excellent service in a peaceful location. Guest rooms are simple but luxurious, with fireplaces, down quilts, and heated slate floors in the bathrooms. The Temple Mountain Spa is the best in Lake Louise. *200 Pipestone Rd.* ☎ *800/661-1586 or 403/522-3989. www.posthotel.com. 92 units. Doubles $345–$850. AE, MC, V. Map p 76.*

A common area inside the Lake Louise Alpine Centre.

Rimrock Resort Hotel BANFF Modern and slick, the Rimrock has a great view and fine lodgings. The lobby is graced by a giant marble fireplace, cherry oak walls, leather chairs, and big windows offering views you can't get even in the penthouses of other local hotels. Peaceful and elegant, rooms are airy, luxurious, and large. Request one on the east face of the south wing for the choicest views. *300 Mountain Ave.* ☎ *800/661-1587 or 403/762-3356. www.rimrockresort.com. 346 units. Doubles $238–$630. AE, MC, V. Map p 76.*

Rundlestone Lodge BANFF There is a long line of mid-size hotels and motels along Banff Avenue. This one stands out because it

A peaceful sitting room at the Post Hotel.

has more of a modern feel. The gym, pool, and the large size of standard rooms add value. Predictable but clean, with bonus points for the very friendly service. *537 Banff Ave.* ☎ *800/661-8630 or 403/762-2201. www.rundlestone. com. 96 rooms. Doubles $164–$294. AE, MC, V. Map p 76.*

★★ **Skoki Lodge** BACKCOUNTRY This is a classic backcountry lodge built nearly a century ago, so you must ski or hike 11km (6.8 miles) to get here, arriving to a gorgeous valley behind the Lake Louise ski area. The lodge is rustic; there is no electricity or running water. There are, however, incredible trails at your doorstep and true Rocky Mountain seclusion. *Banff National Park.* ☎ *800/258-7669. www.skoki lodge.com. Sleeps up to 22 guests. From $225 per person including meals. AE, MC, V. Map p 76.*

Storm Mountain Lodge BANFF OUTSKIRTS A collection of old-fashioned cabins halfway between Banff and Lake Louise have been nicely restored with large tubs, crackling fireplaces, and comfy beds. Unit nos. 9 and 10 are farthest from the sometimes-noisy Hwy. 93. Nos. 11 and 14 have great views of Castle Mountain. *On Hwy. 93 just west of Castle Junction.* ☎ *403/762-4155. www.storm mountainlodge.com. 14 units. Cabins $169–$239. MC, V. Map p 76.*

Travel Tip

Remember that sites at Lake Louise (tent and trailer) and at all Tunnel Mountain campgrounds should be reserved in advance at www. pccamping.ca. All other sites are on a first-come, first-served basis.

Sunshine Mountain Lodge

SUNSHINE VILLAGE Banff's only ski-in/ski-out hotel is located at the top of the gondola at Sunshine Village ski resort. Rooms are luxurious, ranging from quite affordable little doubles to spacious two-story suites. The biggest bonus? You get fresh tracks each morning. Open winter only. *1 Sunshine Rd.* ☎ *403/ 705-4000. www.sunshinemountain lodge.com. 84 rooms. Ski and stay packages start at $164/person. AE, MC, V. Map p 76.*

Tunnel Mountain Village Campground

BANFF You can walk to Banff Avenue from the park's biggest campground. It's divided into three sections: a mixed tent and RV camp 2.5km (1½ miles) east of town, an RV mecca 4km (2½ miles) east of town, and a trailer- and tenter-friendly section to the east of the RV area. *4km (2½ miles) east of Banff Townsite on Tunnel Mountain Rd. Reservations at www. pccamping.ca.* ☎ *877/737-3783. Tunnel Mountain Village I: 618 sites.*

Big windows are a feature of rooms at the Rimrock Resort Hotel.

The oTENTiks at Two Jack Campground are a cross between a tent and an A-frame cabin.

No RV hookups. $27. Closed Oct. 2–May 7. Tunnel Mountain Village II: 188 sites. Electrical hookups only. $32. AE, MC, V. Open year-round. Tunnel Mountain Trailer Court: 321 sites. Full hookups. $38. Closed Oct 2–May 7. AE, MC, V. Map p 76.

Two Jack Campground MINNE-WANKA LOOP There are two areas here. The main area (which is larger and busier) is just off the road in a densely wooded forest 13km (8 miles) northeast of Banff Townsite, on the Minnewanka Loop. It's quite private, although there are no great views. The second area is next to the lake and is very popular since it is the most scenic and peaceful campground near the Town of Banff. The lakeside campground also boasts 10 oTENTiks, a unique cross between a tent and an A-frame cabin, which will appeal to first-time campers and families. Far from luxurious, they are homey,

comfortable, warm, dry, and low maintenance. 12km (7½ miles) from Banff Townsite on Minnewanka Loop Rd. Reservations at www.pccamping. ca. ☎ 877/737-3783. Two Jack Main: 380 sites. RV-friendly but no RV hookups. $22. Closed Sept 9–May 4. Two Jack Lakeside: 74 sites. No RV hookups. $27. Closed Sept 15–May 14. AE, MC, V. Map p 76.

Waterfowl Lake Campground ICEFIELDS PARKWAY This is my favorite in the park because of the scenery and peacefulness. There is an open area on the lakeshore for relaxing or playing games, plus amazing views of the surrounding mountains and glaciers. 57km (35 miles) north of Lake Louise on the Icefields Pkwy., Hwy. 93. No reservations. 116 sites. No RV hookups. $22. Closed Sept 8–June 18. No credit cards. Map p 76.

New Twist on Camping

New to camping but keen to give it a try? Banff's oTENTiks are part-cabin, part-tent that require no set-up. The setting, at Two Jack Lakeside, is also fabulous. There's lighting, electricity, indoor heat, and plenty of room for families up to six. Fun! They're $120 per night. Reserve ahead of time at www.reservation.pc.gc.ca.

Banff Shopping, Arts & Nightlife

Shopping
Banff Tea Company **9**
Banff Wine Store **12**
The Bay **17**
Cabin 108 **24**
Chocolaterie Bernard
    Callebaut **19**
Lammle's Western Wear
    and Tack **2**
Monod's **18**
Philippe of Banff **20**
Qiviuk **27**
Rocks & Gems **14**
Roots **5**
Rude Girls **13**
Soul Ski & Bike **8**
Wilson's **1**

Nightlife
Aurora Nightclub **22**
Banff Ave. Brewing
    Company **23**
The Banff Rose
    and Crown **11**
Bear Street Tavern **7**
Buffalo Paddock **16**
Hoodoo Lounge **15**
Saint James's Gate **4**
Tommy's Neighbourhood
    Pub **21**
Wild Bill's Legendary
    Saloon **10**

Arts & Entertainment
The Banff Centre **25**
Banff Ideas Bank **7**
Bowling at Fairmont
    Banff Springs **26**
Evening Wildlife Safari **6**
Lux Theatre **3**

••• *Walking Path*

Shopping & Nightlife
Best Bets

Best **Cowboy Culture**
★ Wild Bill's, *201 Banff Ave. (p 90)*;
and Lammle's Western Wear,
317 Banff Ave. (p 87)

Best **Dance Floor**
Aurora, *110 Banff Ave. (p 89)*

Best **Outdoor Fashion**
Monod's, *129 Banff Ave. (p 87)*

Best **Ski Shop**
Soul Ski & Bike, *203A Bear St.
(p 88)*

Best **Ladies' Fashion**
Cabin 108, *108 Banff Ave. (p 86)*

Best **for Singles**
Hoodoo, *137 Banff Ave. (p 90)*

Best **Jazz**
★★★ Banff Centre, *107 Tunnel
Mountain Rd. (p 88)*

Best **Low-Key Après Ski**
Tommy's Neighbourhood Pub,
120 Banff Ave. (p 90)

Best **Selection of Beer on Tap**
★ Saint James's Gate, *205 Wolf St.
(p 90)*

Best **Wine and Tapas**
Bear Street Tavern, *211 Bear St.
(p 70)*

Cowboy hats at Lammle's Western Wear and Tack.

Shopping, Arts & Nightlife
A to Z

Shopping

Banff Tea Company BANFF
With more than 180 teas from around the world, from oolong to souchong, you'll sure to find something to keep your thermos tasty while you're out exploring the Rockies. The Rocky Mountain Blend has two kinds of black teas and some Rooibos. Brought to you by the same folks that run the Plain of the Six Glaciers Teahouse (p 84), a portion of proceeds are donated to local charities. *208 Caribou St.* ☎ *403/762-8322. www.banffteaco. com. AE, MC, V. Map p 84.*

Banff Wine Store BANFF The staff at this basement-level shop is incredibly knowledgeable and friendly. Ask for tips on a post-hike pinot or an après-ski cabernet. There are labels from more than a dozen countries and a wide price range, including Canadian ice wine. They also deliver to your hotel! *302 Caribou St.* ☎ *403/782-3465. AE, MC, V. Map p 84.*

The Bay BANFF The Hudson's Bay Company is a Canadian institution established in 1670. Today, the Bay sells everything from cosmetics to Cuisinarts in their three-level department store. Souvenirs here include maple candies, the famous Hudson's Bay blankets, and Olympic uniforms. *125 Banff Ave.* ☎ *403/762-5525. www.hbc.com. AE, DC, MC, V. Map p 84.*

Cabin 108 BANFF An independently owned fashion boutique that has plenty of finds at good prices, come here to pick up a new outfit before hitting the clubs or wine bars later. *108 Banff Ave.* ☎ *403/ 762-2108. AE, MC, V. Map p 84.*

Chocolaterie Bernard Callebaut BANFF This Belgian-born Calgarian is a fifth-generation chocolate maker who says he eats at least six different chocolates each day. His Banff store, inside the Harmony Lane Mall, is practically an education in all things chocolate. Choose from 48 flavors, including

Some of the delectables for sale at Chocolaterie Bernard Callebaut.

Seashell
hazelnut paste

Caraques
Milk

Manon
marzipan, walnut, meringue

Colorful towels, tote bags, and more on display at the Bay.

dark chocolate-coated ginger, ganache cream, and truffles. *111 Banff Ave.* ☎ *403/762-4106. www.bernardcallebaut.com. AE, MC, V. Map p 84.*

Lammle's Western Wear and Tack BANFF   For true-blue cowboy gear, head upstairs in Cascade Plaza. Start with a Shady Brady cowboy hat and a pair of Wrangler jeans with a silver belt; then wrap up the whole outfit up with a pair of Dan Post cowboy boots. They also have kidswear for junior saddle ropers. *Cascade Plaza, 317 Banff Ave.* ☎ *403/762-5460. www.lammles. com. AE, MC, V. Map p 84.*

Monod's BANFF   Banff's oldest outdoor clothing and equipment retailer is a busy, jam-packed shop staffed by keen outdoorsy types. Hiking boots are upstairs at the back, along with fly-fishing rods, while climbing harnesses and tents are downstairs, and cold-weather wear right in the middle. Fleeces, puffy vests or zip-off pants, anyone? *129 Banff Ave.* ☎ *403/762-4571. www.monodsports.com. AE, MC, V. Map p 84.*

Philippe of Banff BANFF   Since Banff is the jewel of the Rockies, it's only appropriate that you'd find some diamonds at this fine jeweler's atelier. Banff goldsmith Philippe Plourde handcrafts stunning jewelry that honors tradition yet embraces modern styles. *130 Banff Ave.* ☎ *403/760-8744. AE, MC, V. Map p 84.*

Qiviuk BANFF   Celebrities have discovered that it's softer than cashmere, warmer than beaver or fox fur, lighter than wool. The supple and plush pelt from the Canadian Arctic musk ox comes from the Far North, making qiviuk the world's rarest natural fiber. This store in the Banff Springs sells sweaters, coats, hats, shawls, and scarves. *Fairmont Banff Springs Hotel, 405 Spray Ave.* ☎ *403/762-4460. www.qiviuk.com. AE, DC, MC, V. Map p 84.*

Rocks and Gems BANFF   Bring the kids to scour the big bin of tumbled stone and bring a small souvenir home with them. There are two giant amethyst geodes on display. *137 Banff Ave.* ☎ *403/762-9330. www.rocksandgemscanada.com. Map p 84.*

Roots BANFF   Canada's iconic leather and casual clothing shop is a great place for a maple-leaf–inspired souvenir, from hoodies to baby sleepers. They've lately started dabbling in yoga wear and linens, but maintain their—um, roots—with sweats. This is your chance to adapt the Canadian lifestyle with genuine leather and always-stylish purses, jackets, and shoes. *277 Banff Ave.* ☎ *403/762-9434. http://canada. roots.com. AE, MC, V. Map p 84.*

Rude Girls BANFF   Every female shredder or ripper needs the clothes and style to go with the big-mountain attitude. This boutique (the sister of Rude Boys, which shares the store) has edgy, punky fashion for girls who like to snowboard, ski, skateboard, surf, or just generally want to look cool. *203 Caribou St.* ☎ *403/762-8211. www. rudeboys.com. AE, MC, V. Map p 84.*

Soul Ski and Bike BANFF   In a town packed with ski shops, this one stands out for their large selection of ski and snowboards in winter and bikes in summer. Plus, the service is friendly, and there's plenty of inspiration here to help get you outside. *203A Bear St.* ☎ *403/760-1640. www.soulskiandbike.com. AE, MC, V. Map p 84.*

Wilson Mountain Sports LAKE LOUISE   Carrying everything from tents and hiking poles to fleeces and snowshoes, this is a great one-stop shop in the village at Lake Louise for all your outdoor needs. Camping, hiking, skiing, climbing, biking—they have almost everything here! *Building A, Samson Mall, 201 Village Rd.* ☎ *403/522-3636. www. wmsll.com. AE, MC, V. Map p 84.*

Arts & Entertainment
★★★ The Banff Centre BANFF   For inspiring concerts featuring world-class jazz, dance, pop, folk, and world music, keep an eye on the calendar and hope something is happening during your visit. *St. Julien Rd.* ☎ *403/762-6301. www. banffcentre.ca. Wed, Fri–Sun 9pm–2am. Admission varies. Map p 84.*

Banff Ideas Bank BANFF   If you are lucky enough to be in town for one of these monthly evening events, don't miss it. Locals and visitors gather for "Conversation Cafes" to discuss issues relevant to living in Banff, such as: how to keep youth in town; what does it mean to live in a national park; and how to make the most of life in Banff. Stirring chatter and friendly faces make this a superb chance to soak up the local scene. *Held at the Wild*

Warm up with a jacket from Monod's.

Dancers perform at the Banff Centre.

Flour Bakery, 211 Bear St., every the first Wed of every month at 7pm. www.banffideasbank.ca. Map p 84.

kids Bowling at Fairmont Banff Springs BANFF

There are four lanes of five-pin bowling at the Fairmont Banff Springs Hotel, which makes for a lively and fun family evening activity, especially on a stormy night. There's also a video game arcade and bar inside. *405 Spray Ave., in the Conference Centre.* ☎ *403/762-6892. www.fairmont. com/banffsprings. $6/game. Mon–Thurs 3–10pm, Fri–Sat 10am–11pm, Sun 1–7pm. Map p 84.*

★ Evening Wildlife Safari

BANFF Two-hour van-based wildlife tours run by Discover Banff Tours depart Banff each evening, taking full advantage of what is perhaps your best bet for wildlife sightings. The guides are very good, and binoculars are provided. *Discover Banff Tours' office is in Sundance Mall, 215 Banff Ave.* ☎ *403/ 760-5007. www.banfftours.com. Adults $40, kids 5–12 $25. Daily at 6:30pm. Map p 84.*

Lux Theatre BANFF

Banff's venerable but aging cinema plays mainly first-run Hollywood hits, and there's always a family-friendly blockbuster running. *229 Bear St.*

☎ *403/762-8595. www.landmark cinemas.ca. Adults $10, children 11 and under $7. Map p 84.*

Nightlife

Aurora Nightclub BANFF

The best spot for later-night dancing and funky techno atmosphere. There's a cigar room, a martini bar, and karaoke on Thursdays. *110 Banff Ave., downstairs.* ☎ *403/760-5300. www.aurorabanff.com. Admission varies $6–$12. Map p 84.*

Banff Ave. Brewing Company

BANFF It's "all about the beer" at this second-story microbrewery, particularly lively in the après-ski, or après-work (yes, people in Banff do work) hours. A sampler lets you try their half-dozen specialties. The menu is staple pub food—try the meatloaf or a huge serving of poutine. *111 Banff Ave., 2nd floor.* ☎ *403/762-1003. www.banff avebrewingco.com. Free admission. Daily 11:30am–2am. Map p 84.*

The Banff Rose and Crown

BANFF With a spacious rooftop patio and a long list of beers on tap, this is a laid-back favorite with a low-brow style. There is often live music, including Maritime Mondays for fans of the East Coast. *202 Banff Ave., upstairs.* ☎ *403/762-2121.*

The bar at Aurora Nightclub.

www.roseandcrown.ca. Admission varies $4–$12. Daily 11am–2am. Map p 84.

Buffalo Paddock Pub BANFF On the top floor of the Mt. Royal Hotel, come for billiards, darts, shuffleboard, foosball, and more than a dozen large-screen TVs. *124 Banff Ave. ☎ 403/760-8543. www. mountroyalhotel.com. Free admission. Daily noon–2am. Map p 84.*

Hoodoo Lounge BANFF Those who really want to party can join the young crowd in the basement here for top-20 dance tunes. Specials practically every night of the week, from ladies' night to live music. *137 Banff Ave. ☎ 403/760-8636. www.hoodoolounge.com. Admission varies $5–$14. Daily 9pm–2am. Closed Wed and Sun. Map p 84.*

★ Saint James's Gate BANFF Inspired by the birthplace of Guinness, selecting a draught here is just about the toughest challenge in Banff—there are 33 beers on tap,

as well as 50 single-malt scotches and 10 Irish whiskeys. Live music is almost always Celtic and a blast. *205 Wolf St. ☎ 403/762-9355. www. stjamesgatebanff.com. Admission varies $4–$14. Daily 11am–2am. Map p 84.*

Tommy's Neighbourhood Pub BANFF Locals here are happy to share stories of what it's like to live in such a storied town. This is a friendly place where you can actually have a conversation without yelling. *120 Banff Ave. ☎ 403/762-8888. www.tommysneighbourhood pub.com. Free admission. Daily 11am–2am. Map p 84.*

★ Wild Bill's Legendary Saloon BANFF The local cowboy hangout is fun and not necessarily all about the yee-haw. What can I say? Head here if you want to drink beer and do some line dancing. Wednesday nights brings line-dance lessons. *201 Banff Ave., upstairs. ☎ 403/762-0333. www.wbsaloon.com. Admission varies $5–$18. Daily 11am–2am. Map p 84.* ●

The Canadian Rockies

Kananaskis Country

Legend	
△	Campground
⛽	Gasoline
✚	Hospital/First Aid
ⓘ	Information
■	Point of Interest
🎿	Ski Resort

1 Barrier Lake Visitors Centre
2 Nakiska
3 Kananaskis Village
4 Fireweed Grill
5 Kananaskis Country Golf Course
6 Peter Lougheed Visitors Centre

Previous Page: Hiking at beautiful Lake O'Hara.

Kananaskis Country is a vast area of rugged mountain wilderness that contains four Alberta provincial parks and "multiple-use" land where forestry, cattle-grazing, and petroleum development are permitted. Roads and trails are quiet here compared to Banff, drawing mainly weekenders from Calgary. Kananaskis is named for a Cree native who was reportedly struck by an axe but survived, and there's a good variety of outdoor activities, gorgeous scenery, and excellent infrastructure.

From Banff, take the Trans-Canada Highway west 55km (34 miles). Turn south on Hwy. 40, the Kananaskis Trail.

❶ Barrier Lake Visitors Centre. This is a good first stop, at the entrance to Kananaskis Country on Hwy. 40. Pick up brochures and maps. ⏱ *15 min. Hwy. 40, 8km (5 miles) south of Trans-Canada Hwy. 1.* ☎ *403/673-3985. May 12–June 28 Mon–Fri 9:30am–4pm, Sat–Sun 9am–5pm; June 29–Sept 3 Fri 8:30am–6pm, Sat–Thurs 8:30am–5pm; Sept 4 to mid-May 9:30am–4pm.*

Continue south on Hwy. 40 for 14km (8⅔ miles). Turn right towards Kananaskis Village, continuing straight for 2.5km (1½ miles).

❷ Nakiska. The site of the alpine skiing events at the 1988 Calgary Winter Olympics, this is a great family ski hill, steps from Kananaskis Village on the lower slopes of Mt. Allan. Pop by for a photo-op beside assorted Olympic paraphernalia.

The chair lift at Nakiska ski resort.

2.5km (1½ miles) from Kananaskis Village on Village Rd. ☎ *403/591-7777. www.skinakiska.com.*

Return back towards Hwy. 40, turning right after 2.5km (1½ miles).

❸ Kananaskis Village. The heart of "K-Country" is home to a golf course, tennis courts, hotels, horse-riding stables, a café, a hotel and conference center currently

The Kananaskis Country Golf Course.

under renovation and plenty of trails. It's a year-round resort hub that offers a pleasant stroll and a handful of shops. *26km (16 miles) south of Trans-Canada Hwy. 1 on Hwy. 40. Turn right on Mt. Allen Dr. and left on Centennial Dr. Follow directions to parking lot.*

4 Fireweed Grill. Pop into the Delta Lodge at Kananaskis, which is undergoing massive renovations beginning in 2016, for lunch at the Fireweed Grill. On a summer day, sit on the patio. There are plenty of pizzas and salads to choose from, but I suggest the indulgent Alberta beef dip, famous in these parts. Call the Grill first to make sure it's not impacted by the renovation. *1 Centennial Dr., Kananaskis Village.* ☎ *403/591-6272. $$.*

Head north out of the Village and then turn left at the first stop sign.

5 Kananaskis Country Golf Course. Two 18-hole, par-72 courses make up one of the top-rated and most scenic golf resorts in Canada. It's undergoing big renovations in 2016 but will be open in 2017. *Clubhouse is on Lorette Dr. south of Kananaskis Village.* ☎ *877/591-2525 or 403/591-7272. www. kananaskisgolf.com. Green fees from $98. Early May to mid-Oct 7am–10pm.*

Mt. Kidd in Peter Lougheed Provincial Park.

Continue south on Hwy. 40 for 30km (19 miles), turn west on Kananaskis Lakes Trail and travel 3.7km (2⅓ miles).

6 Peter Lougheed Provincial Park. Easy interpretive trails lead out from an excellent visitors center onto the shores of the lovely Upper and Lower Kananaskis Lakes. A more demanding hike goes up from the peninsula in between the two lakes to Mt. Indefatigable for superb valley views (hiking boots a must!). Mountain bikers come for the Pocaterra Trail. ☎ *403/591-6322. June–Sept 9am–8pm; Oct–May Mon–Thurs 9:30am–4:30pm, Fri–Sat 9am–5pm.*

Chinook Country

Don't be surprised by quick and drastic rises in temperatures during wintertime here. When warm Pacific air comes funneling through to the foothills and slams into a cold high pressure air mass, dry air is compressed and heated, dropping quickly and producing a phenomenon known as a chinook. Local temperatures can go up as much as 40°C (72°F) in 20 minutes. Most winters bring 20 chinook days a year to the eastern edge of the Canadian Rockies near Kananaskis Country.

Canmore

1. Grassi Lakes
2. Good Earth Coffee Co.
3. Canmore Geoscience Museum
4. Avens Gallery
5. Bow River Walk
6. Harvest
7. Canmore Nordic Centre Provincial Park

••• Walking Path

It's hard to beat Canmore. The town of 12,000 boasts beautiful scenery, world-class trails, plus a relatively short commute to Banff or Calgary. Mountains rise high in all directions, and the turquoise Bow River flows through town. Locals take pride in healthy living, the great cafes and restaurants, and the keen arts scene that have earned Canmore the nickname of "Alberta's Aspen." Many visitors stay here for hotel rates that are typically lower than in Banff, making it a good place to begin day trips into the park. The best way to explore Canmore is on foot.

At the west end of Main Street, turn left and drive over the Bow River. Turn left again at Three Sisters Drive and right onto Spray Lakes Road. One kilometer (⅔ mile) past the Nordic Centre, turn left into a parking lot for the trail head.

1 ★★ **Grassi Lakes.** Start the day with a moderate, short but stunning hike just above town. It's a 4km (2.5-mile) loop that takes you up historic steps, past a waterfall and on to two small, jewel-like lakes. *Just past Nordic Centre on the Smith Dorrien-Spray Lakes Rd.*

Head back down the hill, around the shore of the reservoir, and into town. Park in the lot behind 8th Street and between ArtsPlace and the Information Centre.

A display at the Canmore Geoscience Museum.

2 Good Earth Coffee Co.

Reward yourself with breakfast on Main Street. There are many places to choose from, but the baked goods and deluxe breakfast sandwiches (and the sunny patio) at this local favorite are real standouts. *718 Main St. ☎ 403/675-1204. Daily 7am–9pm. $.*

Around the corner to the right, staying on the same block, and inside the Civic Centre is:

3 Canmore Geoscience Museum.

From coal mining to Olympic fame, there's human as well as geological history to discover in this museum. It is housed in Canmore's Civic Centre, which has won awards for its eco-friendly design. *902b 7th Ave. ☎ 403/678-2462. www.cmags.org. Admission $5 adults, $3 students and seniors. Summer Mon–Tues noon–5pm, Wed–Sun 10am–5pm; Sept 5–May 17 Mon–Fri noon–5pm, Sat–Sun 11am–5pm.*

Stroll back to the left along Main Street for window shopping. On the south side is the:

4 Avens Gallery.

For 20 years, this has been the premier art gallery in Canmore. There's small art (jewelry, sculpture, blown glass), but the most impressive are the large canvases representing the inspiring local scenery. Also check out Elevation Gallery a few doors up the road. *104–709 Main St. ☎ 403/678-4471. Wed–Sun 11am–5pm.*

Continue down Main Street and keep straight as Main Street becomes Riverview Place. At the far end of the cul-de-sac, a sign marks the beginning of a walking trail.

Walkers cross a bridge over the Bow River.

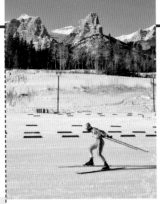

⑤ Bow River Walk. At the end of Main Street, follow footpath signs to the Bow River Walk, which traces both sides of this turquoise alpine river while taking in dazzling mountain scenery. A gentle 30-minute loop takes you over the old railway bridge, past the TransAlta Plant, and back to town over Bridge Road.

Return to Main Street, turning left on 7th Avenue and right on 10th Street.

⑥ ★ Harvest. This is where locals grab a healthy and hearty lunch. Most sandwiches are grilled, croque monsieur–style. On Sundays, there are homemade cinnamon buns. It's just off Main Street. *718 10th St. ☎ 403/678-3747. Daily 8:30am–3pm. $.*

Get back in the car and retrace your route up towards Grassi Lakes. Take a right at the large signs.

⑦ Canmore Nordic Centre Provincial Park. The park was the

A skier at the Canmore Nordic Centre.

host of the Nordic skiing and biathlon events for the 1988 Calgary Winter Olympics and is the only Canadian stop on the Nordic World Cup tour. There are more than 65km (40 miles) of ski trails in winter, 100km (62 miles) of mountain-bike trails in summer, and a Frisbee golf course. *1.8km (1 mile) south of Canmore, take Rundle Dr. across the Bow River Bridge, go left at Three Sisters Dr. and right at Spray Lakes Rd.; follow signs. ☎ 403/678-2400.*

Extreme Golf in the Rockies

There are three outstanding golf courses at Canmore. The oldest course in town is the friendly 18-hole **Canmore Golf and Curling Club** (2000 8th Ave.; ☎ 403/678-4785; www.canmoregolf.net) close to downtown, along the Bow River. Greens fees are $80 per person. The clubhouse has one of the best patios in town. On the north side of Canmore is **SilverTip Resort** (1000 SilverTip Trail, exit at the main Canmore exit and take first left before the lights; ☎ 877/877-5444 or 403/678-1600; www.silvertipresort.com). Calling what it offers "extreme mountain golf," this Les Furber–designed 18-hole, par-72 course is one of a kind. Greens fees range from $125 to $175. **Stewart Creek Golf Course** (1 Stewart Creek Rd., via the Three Sisters Pkwy. exit just east of Canmore; ☎ 877/993-4653 or 403/609-6099; www.stewartcreekgolf.com) is another "high mountain" course that winds along the picturesque lower slopes of the Three Sisters Mountain on the south side of the Bow Valley. Greens fees range from $129 to $195.

Icefields Parkway (Jasper)

0 | 10 mi
0 | 10 km

Hinton

Brule Lake

Indian River

Park Gate

16

Snaring River Campground

Pyramid Lake
Patricia Lake
Lake Annette

Medicine Lake

Jasper

JASPER NATIONAL PARK

Wapiti Campground

Ski Marmot Basin

Whistlers Campground
Wabasso Campground

93A

Maligne River

finish here

Mount Edith Cavell

93

Maligne Lake

Mount Christie

Athabasca River

Icefields

93

Sunwapta River

Chaba Icefield

Columbia Icefield

start here

To Lake Louise, Banff

Legend:
- ⛺ Campground
- ✚ Hospital/First Aid
- ⓘ Information
- ◼ Point of Interest
- 🎿 Ski Area

Area of map (inset)
Edmonton
ALBERTA
Jasper
Lake Louise
Golden
Banff
Calgary
BRITISH COLUMBIA
CANADA
UNITED STATES
40 16 93 2

1. The Columbia Icefield
2. The Glacier Experience
3. Glacier Skywalk
4. Sunwapta Falls
5. Highway 93A
6. Athabasca Falls
7. Cavell Road
8. Mount Edith Cavell
9. Path of the Glacier Trail

As you drive north on the Icefields Parkway, Hwy. 93, you enter Jasper National Park, the largest of the national parks in the Canadian Rockies at 10,878 sq. km (4,200 sq. miles). Large carnivores roam the wide valleys here, so drive slowly and keep an eye out for wildlife; the scenery sometimes more closely resembles the moon than the Rocky Mountains. This tour only covers the highway north of the Icefields Centre; for information on the southern half of the Parkway, see p 64.

❶ ★★★ The Columbia Icefield.

The geographical heart of the Icefields Parkway is a world-class natural wonder and living laboratory that examines glaciology and mountain geology. It's fantastically visitor-friendly, and is located just north of the Banff National Park border, some 103km (64 miles) south of the Town of Jasper. There is a Parks Canada Information Centre inside the Icefields Centre that is open May through late September only, while the building itself is open early April through mid-October. ☎ 780/852-6288.

❷ ★★ The Glacier Experience.

The venerable Brewster family operates giant "snocoaches" that take you right on to the Athabasca Glacier, giving you a sense of the enormity of this icefield. You get about 15 minutes to walk on top of the 300m- (984-ft.) thick sheets of ice. Although coaches leave every 15 minutes, the tours can be very busy, especially in summer, so reservations are highly recommended. ☎ 403/762-6735. www.explore rockies.com. Adults $50, kids 6–15 $25, free for kids 5 and under.

Apr 6–30 and Oct 1–18 10am–4pm; May 1–31 and Sept 1–30 9am–5pm; June 1–Aug 31 9am–6pm.

Drive north on the Icefields Parkway for 9km (5½ miles)

❸ ★ Glacier Skywalk. A new
lookout walkway that will likely take your breath away is definitely worth the stop. It's a glass-bottomed walkway with a 918-foot drop offering spectacular views over this ancient landscape, and a chance to spot wildlife. There's plenty of interpretive information provided as well. This tour starts from the Icefields Centre; you can't drive yourselves there. It includes bus transfers. 96km (60 miles) from Jasper and 9km (5½ miles) from the Icefields Centre. ☎ 866/606-6700. www.brewster.ca. Adults $31, kids 6–15 $15. Mid-Apr to end Apr 10am–4pm; May 10am–5pm; June 10am–6pm; July–Aug 10am–7pm; Sept 10am–5:30pm; Oct 1 to mid-Oct 10am–4pm, weather permitting.

Continue north on the Icefields Parkway for 41km (25 miles).

❹ Sunwapta Falls. The Sunwapta River tumbles through a steep-walled

The patio at the Icefields Centre yields great views of the Columbia Icefield.

An aerial view of Sunwapta Falls.

limestone gorge, making a sharp turn from northwest to southwest. Follow a 2km (1.2-mile) trail along the north bank of the river for excellent views. *50km (31 miles) north of Icefields Centre and 55km (34 miles) south of Jasper Townsite. Follow turnoff to parking lot.*

Continue north on the Icefields Parkway, turning northwest or left onto:

5 **Hwy. 93A.** The Icefields Parkway soon meets Hwy. 93A, a scenic road with less traffic that heads up towards Jasper. It's a good option if you have time. *30km (19 miles) from Jasper and 75km (47 miles) from Icefields Centre.*

Make a quick left into the parking lot at:

6 ★ **Athabasca Falls.** The milky-blue Athabasca River pours through a narrow canyon cut out of quartzite rock. A nearby bridge offers phenomenal views of the thundering falls and Mt. Kerkeslin in the background. *Just past the 93A turnoff, on south side of road, 30km (19 miles) south of Jasper and 75km (47 miles) north of the Icefields Centre.*

Continue northwest on 93A. After 8km (5 miles), turn left.

7 ★ **Cavell Road.** Follow Hwy. 93A north along the west bank of

the Athabasca River and over the Whirlpool River to Cavell Road. Turn left. Completed in 1924, this narrow, winding road is challenging to drive, and is off-limits to most RVs and trailers (anything over 7m/23 ft.). It is also closed from October through June, depending on snow.

8 **Mt. Edith Cavell.** At 3,363m (11,033 ft.), Mt. Edith Cavell, named after a World War I heroine, is the highest and arguably most scenic mountain in the vicinity of Jasper Townsite. Angel Glacier saddles the northeastern slope and sends a tongue of ice off the cliffside. *28km (17 miles) from Hwy. 93A on the Cavell Rd.*

9 ★★ **The Path of the Glacier Trail.** From the parking lot at the base of Mt. Edith Cavell, this trail takes you over boulders, shrubbery, pebbles, and sand through a landscape which, less than a century ago, was covered by a glacier. New plants, trees, shrubs, and wildflowers have slowly returned to the area, known as a terminal moraine. *It's an easy 1.6km (1-mile) loop that will take 45 min.*

Drive back down the Cavell Road and turn left on Hwy. 93A, which will take you back to Jasper.

Mt. Edith Cavell.

Maligne Valley Road

1 Maligne Canyon

2 Maligne Lake Cruise
to Spirit Island

3 Curly Phillips' Boathouse

4 Mary Schaffer Loop

This road takes you through the Maligne Valley and ends at
the picturesque Maligne Lake. Wildlife can often be spotted on
this half-day outing, including bighorn sheep, deer, elk, moose,
grizzly bear, and black bear. With a handful of stops, some short
hikes, and a boat cruise, it will take you most of the day. START:
Town of Jasper.

Drive east on Connaught Street,
turning left onto Hwy. 16. After
4km (2½ miles), turn south onto
Maligne Lake Road.

1 **Maligne Canyon.** A spectacular example of the cutting power of
moving water, this is a very long,
gradual waterfall through a deep
limestone canyon. There are a
series of bridges that take you back
and forth down the canyon. *2.3km
(1.4 miles) on the Maligne Lake Rd.
to Sixth Bridge parking lot.*

Continue on the Maligne Lake
Road to its end.

2 ★★ kids **Maligne Lake
Cruise to Spirit Island.** This is
the best boat tour in the Canadian
Rockies. From the deck of the
glass-enclosed boats (which are
heated on chilly days), watch for
eagles, mountain goats, and even
the odd avalanche. The cruise
makes a stop halfway up the lake at
the mysterious Spirit Island, then
returns to the dock. *At the end of
Maligne Lake Rd.* ☎ *866/625-4463
or 780/852-3370. www.malignelake.
com. Adults $55, kids 5–14 $28.
Cruises depart hourly in summer
10am–5pm.*

Looking down at Maligne Canyon.

❸ Curly Phillips' Boathouse.

Curly Phillips, a canoe guide and trapper from Ontario, built a floating boathouse on Maligne Lake in 1928 that still stands today. Rent canoes at this historic building for $30 an hour. *Just east of the cafeteria behind the first parking lot on Maligne Lake.* ☎ 780/852-3370.

❹ Mary Schaffer Loop (also

known as Loop Trail). A pleasant hike around the north side of Maligne Lake, the largest lake in the Canadian Rockies, reaches a viewpoint with an interpretive display about explorer Mary Schaffer, the first woman of European descent to set eyes on the lake, in 1908, and the most prolific writer about the place. It's a 3.2km (2-mile) loop that will take you just over an hour.

East of Jasper

Miette Hot Springs ★. Head out for one of Jasper's best hikes (the Sulphur Skyline), then soak your tired bones in these hot mineral pools. From Jasper Townsite, follow the Yellowhead Hwy. 16, 42km (26 miles) east to Miette Road. Follow Miette Road 17km (11 miles) south to the end of the road. ☎ 780/866-3939. *Adults $6, seniors and children $5, family pass $18. Mid-May to 3rd week of June and early Sept to mid-Oct 10:30am–9pm; late June to early Sept 8:30am–10:30pm. Closed mid-Oct to mid-May.*

Soaking in Miette Hot Springs.

Town of Jasper

Legend:
- Hospital/First Aid
- P Parking

Pyramid Ave.
Geikie
Patricia
Connaught Dr.
Pyramid Lake Rd.
Elm
Pyramid Bench
Miette Ave.
Hazel Ave.
Geikie
Patricia
Connaught Dr.
Athabasca River
93A
16
Miette River
93
To Banff

0 ——— 1/4 mi
0 ——— 1/4 km

1. Jasper National Park Information Centre
2. Heritage Railway Station
3. Jasper Skytram
4. Patricia St. Deli
5. Jasper-Yellowhead Museum
6. Old Fort Point
7. Pyramid and Patricia Lakes

Located in the heart of the park, the town of Jasper came into being in anticipation of a transcontinental railway that now runs up the Athabasca Valley and over the Yellowhead Pass. The Canadian National Railway built a series of cabins on the shores of Lac Beauvert, which later became the Jasper Park Lodge. Today, the town feels very different from the Town of Banff—it's less crowded, more laid-back and lacks the swanky shops and nightclubs of its southern counterpart.

1 Jasper National Park Information Centre. In this cozy and central heritage building, get your bearings and get information from the Friends of Jasper, Parks Canada, and Jasper Tourism and Commerce, all of which have booths at the information center. Jasper Tourism and Commerce can tell you about hotel, restaurant, and outfitting options in the park (☎ 780/852-3858). *500 Connaught Dr.* ☎ *780/852-6176. Mar 1 to mid-May 9am–5pm; mid-May to June 12 and* *Oct 1–31 9am–5pm; June 13–Aug 31 8:30am–7pm; Sept 1–30 9am–6pm; Nov 1–Apr 4 9am–5pm.*

Cross Connaught Street to visit the:

2 Heritage Railway Station. Like the CIBC Bank building next to the Info Centre, this building is a great example of the rustic Arts and Crafts architecture of its era. Built in 1921 and designated a World Heritage Site in 1991, it now houses park administration as well as the train station. You can still

The Jasper National Park Information Centre.

picture Victorian ladies with their parasols and elaborate dresses mixing with rough 'n' tumble gold diggers at this old frontier outpost. In fact, many people still arrive in Jasper here via the ViaRail passenger train. *607 Connaught Dr.*

Drive south 4km (2½ miles) from the townsite, on Hwy. 93A, turn west at Whistlers Road and continue for 2.5km (1½ miles) to the

The Jasper-Yellowhead Museum is a great escape on a rainy day.

Tramway terminal, following clearly marked signs to:

❸ ★★ kids Jasper Skytram. Your quickest and easiest way to the high alpine terrain, this 7-minute gondola ride takes you up 973m (3,192 ft.), just short of the summit of the Whistlers. From the top, the views of the Athabasca and Miette valleys are stunning. There's a well-marked, though quite steep, 45-minute trail to the summit of the mountain. The view is more outstanding with each step upward. Dress warmly and wear good walking shoes. At the summit, the panoramic view takes in six mountain ranges, including Mt. Robson, the highest point in the Canadian Rockies. Rides leave every 10 minutes or so. ☎ *780/852-3093. www.jaspertramway.com. Adults $37, children 6–15 $19, free for children 5 and under. Late Mar to mid-May 10am–5pm; mid-May to late June 9am–6pm; late-June to early Sept 9am–8pm; early Sept to mid-Oct 10am–5pm. Closed mid-Oct to mid-May.*

Return to town by the same route. Park on Patricia Street.

4 Patricia St. Deli. The best sandwiches—and some of the friendliest people—in Jasper are at this deli right in the heart of town. "Two slices of bread with heaven in between," they say. A hiker's lunch includes chips and cookies for $13 and makes a great picnic. *606 Patricia St.* 780/852-4814. *$.*

Turn left on Pyramid Avenue and left again on Pyramid Lake Road.

5 Jasper–Yellowhead Museum. Good for a rainy day, this museum has exhibits with artifacts from the park's early days, including fur-trade and mountaineering equipment. You'll find legendary guide Curly Phillips's hand-built cedar-strip canoe, Métis beaded deerskin jackets, and the gear used during the first ascent of Mt. Alberta in 1925. *400 Pyramid Lake Rd.* 780/852-3013. *www.jaspermuseum.org. Adults $6; seniors, students, and children 6–18 $5; free for children 5 and under. Daily 10am–5pm in summer. In winter, closed Mon–Wed.*

Drive 5 minutes south of Jasper Townsite via Hwy. 93A or Hazel Avenue, crossing Hwy. 16. Turn east on Old Fort Point Road and park in the first parking lot after the bridge.

6 ★★ Old Fort Point. Climbing the stairs up Old Fort Point is steep, but worthwhile. Jutting out into the Athabasca River, the point offers great views that take in Jasper Townsite, Lac Beauvert, and the Fairmont Jasper Park Lodge. From here you can also catch sight of Mts. Kerkeslin and Hardisty to the southeast, and the snowy triangle of Mt. Edith Cavell, shining above all others, to the south. The trail head is just across the river bridge on Old Fort Point Road.

Head back to town, east (right) on Connaught Drive and north (left) on Pyramid Lake Road.

7 Pyramid and Patricia Lakes. Head out in the early evening to spot wildlife on land (elk, deer, and moose) and in the water (beavers and ducks) just above town. Fishing is also a draw. Pyramid Island has a nice, short interpretive loop, great for watching the day come to an end.

The stairs up to Old Fort Point.

Yoho National Park

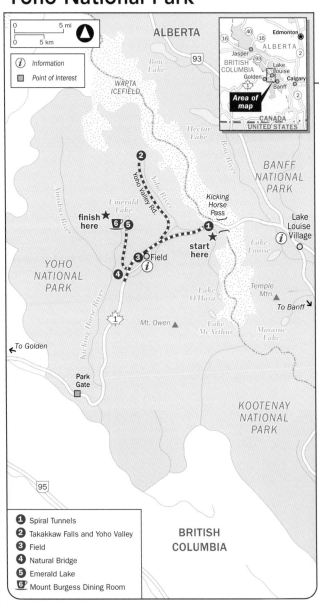

1 Spiral Tunnels
2 Takakkaw Falls and Yoho Valley
3 Field
4 Natural Bridge
5 Emerald Lake
6 Mount Burgess Dining Room

Yoho National Park makes a great base for exploring the Rockies. You're midway between the Columbia Icefield and the Town of Banff, next door to Lake Louise, and yet in a less traveled area. "Yoho" is an expression of awe and wonder in the Cree language, and that's just what you'll experience in the park. This drive takes you from Lake Louise southwest on the Trans-Canada Hwy. 1 through the park toward Golden, British Columbia.

Take the Trans-Canada Hwy. 1 west from Lake Louise 9.2km (5¾ miles) to the border between Alberta and British Columbia. Continue 8.7km (5½ miles) west of the border and turn off into the roadside interpretive display at the:

❶ ★ Spiral Tunnels. The first trains to make it over Kicking Horse Pass had really difficult ascents going toward Lake Louise, or wild rides descending the steep west slope. Engineers developed a groundbreaking plan to ease the incline: the Spiral Tunnels take trains through two loops inside Cathedral Mountain, easing the steepness substantially. View the Spiral Tunnels from two lookouts: The first (and best) is on the side of Trans-Canada Hwy. 1 just up the hill from Field and has excellent interpretive signs; the second is on Yoho Valley Road just past the Cathedral Mountain Lodge.

Continue down the hill on the Trans-Canada Highway another 3.7km (2⅓ miles), turning right at Yoho Valley Road. Continue on to the end.

❷ ★★ Takakkaw Falls and the Yoho Valley. If you love waterfalls, you've come to the right place: "Takakkaw" means magnificent in Cree. At 380m (1,247 ft.), this is the fourth highest waterfall in Canada and originates at the Daly Glacier high above. There's a great picnic spot at the base. Looking to the north, you can often see the Yoho Glacier on a clear day. This is also the trail head for some superb hiking, ranging from an hour to Laughing Falls to 4 hours on the Iceline Trail.

Drive back out to the Trans-Canada Hwy. 1, continuing 1.8km (1 mile) west to the turnoff for Field.

❸ ★ Field. This tiny town is the service center for Yoho National Park. It makes a good place to stop for lunch but isn't worth a visit in

Relaxing in front of Takakkaw Falls.

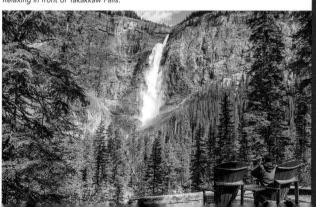

Lake O'Hara: Getting to Paradise

In Yoho National Park, the best hiking trails are at magical Lake O'Hara, a region that makes some locals misty-eyed just at its mention. There are some easy, shorter hikes around the lake itself, and a handful of excellent 3- to 6-hour trails that take you above Lake O'Hara to some of the equally spectacular surrounding lakes. The best bet is to connect all the short hikes into a challenging day hike known as the ★★★ **Lake O'Hara Alpine Circuit** (p 4).

Just on the other side of Lake Louise, O'Hara is accessed by a 13km (8-mile) road that can be hiked or cross-country skied in the winter. But daily Parks Canada–run bus rides (from mid-June to mid-Oct) will take you up to the warden station on the shores of Lake O'Hara in a painless 15 minutes. That'll give you the rest of the day for hiking. You must reserve a spot on the bus by calling ☎ **250/343-6433.** Do this well ahead of time (reservations are accepted beginning Apr 1) because the bus fills up completely—space is very limited. There are no restrictions on the number of people hiking the somewhat boring access road.

While you're on the line, you can also reserve a campsite at the Lake O'Hara Campground if you plan on staying the night at the lake. It's a good spot for families—it's in the backcountry, but accessible by bus so you don't have to worry about carrying everything in on your back.

Bus tickets cost $15 for adults and $7 for children, round-trip. Buses leave the parking lot daily at 8:30 and 10:30am. The last bus out departs the campground at 6:30pm.

The parking lot is located 1km (½ mile) west of the Alberta–British Columbia border, just off the south side of the Trans-Canada Hwy. 1. Turn south at the sign to Lake O'Hara and west into the parking lot. You must reserve campsites well in advance; the reservation line opens April 1. For more information, visit www.pc.gc.ca/yoho. Lake O'Hara Lodge has its own private bus service for its guests (p 137).

Hiking on the Lake O'Hara Alpine Circuit.

and of itself. Grab a sandwich, a coffee, and maybe pop into the pottery shop and keep moving.

Turn left (west) on the Trans-Canada Highway and continue 2km (1¼ miles) to the turnoff for Emerald Lake Road.

❹ Natural Bridge. Just south of Field is the Natural Bridge, where the Kicking Horse River meets with U-shaped sedimentary rock that has so far kept the river from breaking open a deep canyon. The river did manage to erode a small canyon of softer rock just upstream from the tougher section, creating a crooked bridge. Visit it soon—it may be gone in a matter of centuries!

Drive 7km (4⅓ mile) until you reach:

❺ ★★ Emerald Lake. Farther up the road from the Natural Bridge is the spectacular glacier-fed Emerald Lake, featuring hiking trails, canoe rentals, horse stables, and the lovely Emerald Lake Lodge (see "Where to Stay in Yoho National

The Kicking Horse River passes underneath the Natural Bridge.

Park," p 137). A visit to Emerald Lake will fill you with wonder, and could fill an album worth of photos.

☕ Mt. Burgess Dining Room. Finish the day on a high note. The seasonal fine dining inside this historic lodge is all about rustic Rocky Mountain cuisine with artistic flair. The menu focuses on local game like elk, bison, and caribou, and there's an award-winning wine list with over 400 labels. *It's part of Emerald Lake Lodge. On Emerald Lake Rd., 8km (5 miles) off Trans-Canada Hwy. 1, at a turnoff 2km (1¼ miles) south of Field. ☎ 250/343-6321. $$$.*

The Burgess Shale

The Rockies' greatest contribution to archaeology is the 515-million-year-old Burgess Shale, a fossil bed discovered at the base of Mt. Stephen. This discovery transformed our understanding of the evolution of life on Earth and gave real examples of the amazing biodiversity that existed before the mass extinction of species—half of the animal groups seen in the shale have since disappeared from Earth. You can get there to see them only on a 6-hour, 6km (3¾ mile) guided hike organized by the Yoho Burgess Shale Foundation. This is a must for archaeology buffs, but you cannot drive to the Burgess Shale or visit it on your own; you must hike in to the site on an official tour with a registered guide. You will not enjoy this trip unless you are quite fit. Kids will enjoy the shorter hike to the Mt. Stephen Fossil Beds.

Reserve in advance at www.burgess-shale.bc.ca or ☎ 800/343-3006 or 250/343-3006. Hike costs $120 adults, $65 students, $25 children 11 and under. It's available Friday through Monday from July 1 through September 15. The group takes only 15 fit hikers on one trip per day.

Golden, British Columbia

1 Eagle's Eye Gondola and Grizzly Bear Refuge

2 Mountain Biking at Kicking Horse Mountain Resort

3 Rafting the Kicking Horse River

4 Bacchus Books

5 Moberly Marshes

Golden is located just off the Trans-Canada Highway (Hwy. 1) at the confluence of the Kicking Horse and Columbia rivers. The small town (pop. 4,200) has been on the verge of a boom for several years as it shifts gears from a resource-based economy to one based on outdoor recreation. This is largely due to Kicking Horse Mountain Resort, frequently ranked as one of the best ski resorts in North America. Although it is not located within Yoho National Park (it's 20km/12 miles west of the park), Golden is the park's major gateway and service center.

1 ★★ **Eagle's Eye Gondola and Grizzly Bear Refuge.** Soar up to 2,350m (7,710 ft.) for a panoramic view of the Rocky and Purcell mountains. Hike the Terminator Ridge. The gorgeous restaurant opens for lunch only in summer. Combine a gondola ride with a visit to the world's largest enclosed and protected grizzly bear refuge near the gondola's base. It's where Boo the grizzly lives and plays. *From Hwy. 95, turn west at blue sign for Kicking Horse Mountain Resort in downtown Golden, 13km (8 miles) uphill.* ☎ *866/754-5425 or 250/439-5424. www.kickinghorseresort.com. Gondola only: $34 adults, $20 youth 13–18 and seniors, $16 kids 12 and under. Grizzly Bear Refuge: $22 adults, $19 seniors, $16 youth 13–17, $11 kids 6–13, free kids 5 and under, open Mon–Fri only. Gondola June 29–Sept 2 daily 10am–4:30pm; June and Sept 10am–2:30pm.*

A resident at the Grizzly Bear refuge.

2 Mountain Biking. When the snow leaves Kicking Horse Mountain Resort, the trails and the lifts are opened to two-wheelers for world-class downhill biking. Stick your bike on the gondola and cruise down twisty single-track trails. *At the base of Kicking Horse Mountain Resort.* ☎ *866/754-5425 or 250/439-5424. www.kickinghorse resort.com. Full-day bike ticket costs $47 for adults, $38 for youth and seniors, $24 for kids 7–12.*

From Kicking Horse Mountain Resort, head back into Golden. Drive through town and up the hill on Trans-Canada Hwy. 1. Twenty-five kilometers (16 miles) from Golden, turn right at the sign for Beaverfoot Lodge.

3 White-Water Rafting. The rapids on the Kicking Horse River are some of the best in British Columbia. You'll dive through narrow canyons and see the valley from a totally different perspective. Plus,

it's buckets of fun! Kootenay River Runners runs a half-day trip along the river. *1km (⅔ mile) west of the western gates of Kootenay National Park.* ☎ *800/599-4399 or 250/347-9210. www.kootenayriverrunners. com. Rates start at $115. Children age 13 and under not permitted.*

Back in Golden, turn right onto 6th Avenue and take a quick left onto 9th Street.

4 Bacchus Books. Sure, the eclectic first floor is chock-a-block with unique (and distracting!) books, but follow your nose upstairs to the cafe and you'll discover fresh baked treats, natural and thick homemade soups, a roasted veggie panini, or a smoked turkey wrap. *409 9th Ave. N.* ☎ *250/344-5600. www.bacchusbooks.ca. $.*

5 kids Moberly Marshes. The Gadsden Provincial Park houses a wetland that stretches for 180 km (112 miles) and is the largest remaining wetlands area in North America. It's home to more than 260 resident and migratory bird species, and you may also spot deer, elk, beavers, muskrats and mink. Bring your binoculars and stroll along the dikes. *10km (6.2 miles) north of Golden along Trans-Canada Hwy. 1.*

White-water rafting on the Kicking Horse River.

Kootenay National Park

Legend:

- △ Campground
- 🛢 Gasoline
- ✚ Hospital/First Aid
- ⓘ Information
- ▢ Point of Interest
- 🎿 Ski Area

1. Fireweed Trail
2. Stanley Glacier
3. Marble Canyon
4. The Paint Pots
5. Kootenay Park Lodge
6. Radium Hot Springs Pools
7. Sinclair Canyon

A drive through Kootenay National Park makes a great day trip from Banff National Park. Established in 1920, the park is quite long and narrow (94km/58 miles long; 8km/5 miles across) and has a remarkably diverse landscape. The main road through the park traverses the scars of the massive 2003 forest fire; two large lightning-caused fires eventually merged and burned 12.6% of the park. It's a quiet park, with some interesting stops along the Banff–Windermere Highway. It'll take you about 90 minutes to drive back from Radium Hot Springs directly to Banff, but this tour runs southwest, starting at the border of Banff National Park.

Trees along the Fireweed Trail.

Take Hwy. 93 west towards British Columbia.

❶ kids Fireweed Trail. Just past the Continental Divide and over the Alberta–British Columbia border, make a stop at the Vermillion Pass to hike the Fireweed Trail, a short 20-minute loop with interpretive signs that explain why natural forest fires are healthy and good for the environment and are no longer suppressed by Parks Canada. *On the south side of Hwy. 93, at the provincial border.*

Continue west on Hwy. 93.

❷ ★★ Stanley Glacier. Taking you from fire to ice in only 2.5km (1½ miles), this is a relatively short and only moderately steep half-day hike on the crest of the Continental Divide. The family-friendly trail takes you up to a hanging valley with a giant glacier clinging to the limestone cliffs at the back. There are impressive views throughout the entire hike. Great in the morning. *On the south side of Hwy. 93, 3.2km (2 miles) past the provincial border.*

Continue west on Hwy. 93.

❸ ★★ Marble Canyon. If it's a hot day, you'll particularly enjoy a short hike at this narrow trail of limestone carved by two retreated glaciers. The farther up the trail you walk, the more impressive the

Water flowing through Marble Canyon.

Vintage cars parked outside the Kootenay Park Lodge.

canyon. It's cool and shady here. And don't be fooled by the name: There is no marble, only white and gray dolomite rock. Kids will find the hike intriguing, but keep an eye on them because the trail can get very slippery. *On the north side of Hwy. 93, 7km (4⅓ miles) past the provincial border.*

Continue west on Hwy. 93.

④ The Paint Pots. A brief and beautiful walk takes you to this fascinating area where First Nations people gathered ocher, an iron-based mineral that was baked, crushed, mixed with grease, and used as a paint for tepees, pictographs, and personal adornment.

There is an excellent, wheelchair-friendly, 30-minute interpretive trail. *On the north side of Hwy. 93, 10km (6¼ miles) past the provincial border.*

⑤ Kootenay Park Lodge. The only place to stop and grab a bite to eat inside Kootenay National Park is at this historic lodge. Try the homemade burgers and "mountain fries." There's a Parks Canada–run information center next door with snacks, maps, and a friendly staff. *Hwy. 93 at Vermillion Crossing, 42km (26 miles) west of Castle Junction, 61km (38 miles) east of Radium Hot Springs.* ☎ 403/762-9196. *www.kootenayparklodge.com.* $$.

Driving through the red cliffs of Sinclair Canyon.

Radium

A small town (population 675) at the southern end of Kootenay National Park, Radium Hot Springs—often simply called Radium—is named for (you guessed it) its famous hot springs, which draw visitors to soak in their supposedly healing waters. The town is essentially a strip of motels and restaurants, but if you explore some of the back roads you'll discover a spectacular setting and bump into more than a few Calgary residents who make this their second home. It's also a good area for golfing and hiking—the **Radium Resort** (☎ 800/667-6444 or 250/347-6200; www.radium resort.com; map p 134) has an 18-hole championship course located along the cliffs that border the Columbia River, or you can hike the Juniper Trail past Sinclair Canyon or the Valley View Trail which starts at Redstreak Campground.

The popular Radium Hot Springs have been in business since 1914.

Continue west on Hwy. 93.

6 ★ Radium Hot Springs Pools. These "sacred mountain waters" have been drawing visitors to the Columbia Valley since 1914. There is one hot pool (104°F/40°C); and a cooler pool (81°F/27°C), both settled in a canyon rich with oxide, giving the walls a permanent orange-sunset look. *3km (1¾ miles) northeast of the Town of Radium on Hwy. 93.* ☎ *800/767-1611 or*

250/347-9485. www.hotsprings.ca. $7 adults, $6 seniors and children. Mid-May to mid-Oct daily 9am–11pm; mid-Oct to mid-May Mon–Fri 1–9pm, Sat–Sun 10am–9pm.

Continue west on Hwy. 93.

7 Sinclair Canyon. Kootenay closes with a bang at the spectacular red cliffs of Sinclair Canyon, which welcome you to the Columbia Valley just after the Radium Hot Springs pools.

Calgary in One Day

Legend
- (i) Information
- C-Train (Light rail)
- · · · · Walking/Biking Path

1/4 mi
1/4 km

1. Calgary Tower
2. Glenbow Museum
3. Stephen Avenue Mall
4. Olympic Plaza
5. Uptown 17th Ave.
6. Analog Coffee
7. Bow River Trail
8. Simmons Building

With over a million people, a vibrant economy, and plenty of personality, Calgary is stepping boldly into its role as the "heart of the New West." Safe, clean, and young, Calgary has an identity that goes beyond white cowboy hats and rodeos. And while hipsters may snicker at the cowboy schtick, it is really authentic here. Western hospitality is legendarily friendly, upbeat, and relaxed. It's a fun and exciting city that is quite simple to discover. With a day or two, you can take in the main sites, and have a bit of time to wander in one of the city's top neighborhoods—Kensington and Inglewood stand out.

The Calgary Tower and the Calgary skyline.

❶ ★★ Calgary Tower. Come here first to get your bearings 191m (627 ft.) in the sky. You can spot the Stampede Grounds and Pengrowth Saddledome (where the NHL's Calgary Flames play) to the southwest, the Bow River winding through town, and the snow-capped Rocky Mountains on the western horizon. *9th Ave. and Centre St.* ☎ *403/266-7171. www.calgarytower.com. Elevator ride $16 adults, $14 seniors, $11 youth 13–17, $7 children 4–12. June–Aug 9am–10pm; Sept–May 9am–9pm.*

Walk 1 block east on 9th Avenue SE, turning left on 1st SE.

❷ Glenbow Museum. The walls and halls of this storied museum downtown tell the story of the West, from the past to the present. Start in the Blackfoot Gallery to learn about First Nations cultures;

A public art installation on the Stephen Avenue Mall.

Olympic Plaza.

then continue on to the Mavericks Gallery, which celebrates today's groundbreakers. *130 9th Ave. SE, at 1st St.* ☎ *403/268-4100. www. glenbow.org. $14 adults, $10 seniors, $9 students and youth. Mon–Sat 9am–5pm, Sun noon–5pm.*

Turn left on 1st Street SE and left again at 8th Avenue SE, also known as Stephen Avenue.

❸ **Stephen Avenue Mall.** A pedestrian avenue that is lined by banks, high-end shops like Holt Renfrew and Birks, lively eateries, and some interesting public art, this is a great spot for lunch. Try **Charcut** (899 Centre St. S; ☎ 403/984-2180) for butcher steaks, the fashionable **Belvedere** (107 8th Ave. SW; ☎ 403/265-9595), or the chic **Blink** (111 8th Ave. SW; ☎ 403/263-5330).

The patio at Prince's Island's River Cafe

Walk past 1st Street SE to the far east end of Stephen Avenue.

❹ **Olympic Plaza.** A public square across the street from Calgary's stately, sandstone Old City Hall is at the eastern end of Stephen Avenue. Built for the medal ceremonies of the 1988 Winter Olympics, this is where Calgarians come to celebrate everything from hockey victories to Reggaefest. In winter, there's an outdoor skating rink. *228 8th Ave. SE.* ☎ *403/268-2489. Free admission.*

From Stephen Avenue, turn left on 1st SW and walk 7 blocks south.

❺ **Uptown 17th Avenue.** Cross south and venture through a gentrifying neighborhood towards the eclectic, funky stretch of 17th Avenue. Fashion boutiques, vintage stores, clubs, coffee shops, and great bistros draw fashionistas, foodies, and those just looking for a nice stroll. *17th Ave. SW btw. 10th St. and 4th St. SW.*

❻ **Analog Coffee.** At the corner of 17th Avenue and 7th Street, stop in here for a steaming latte. Espresso milkshakes will also pick you up. *740 17 Ave. SW.* ☎ *403/265-2112. $.*

Hop in a cab or turn left at 4th Street SW and walk north 13 blocks, turning right on 2nd Avenue SW.

7 Bow River Trail. This wide, paved pathway is where Calgarians come to walk, run, bike, push strollers, inline skate, and get fresh air. Rent a bike at **Rapid Rent** (from $10/hr., in the Eau Claire Market, Barclay Parade SW, ☎ 403/444-5845; www.rapidrent.ca) then ride or walk from the 9th Street pedestrian bridge downriver as far as the George C. King Bridge near the zoo.

Stop in for a drink and food at

8 Simmons Building. Inside a recently refurbished historic warehouse on the river banks, you'll find some of Calgary's finest food. There's the outstanding **Sidewalk Citizen Bakery, Phil & Sebastian Coffee Roasters,** and the **Charbar** restaurant (p. 123). It's the heart of the up-and-coming East Village neighborhood development. *Confluence Way, near 2nd Ave. SW and 3rd St. SW.*

Then bike over the George C. King pedestrian bridge, back on the north side of the river, completing the loop by crossing the Peace Bridge.

Stampede

If you're in Calgary during the first 2 weeks of July, well, yeehaw! The world-famous Calgary Stampede, calling itself the "Greatest Outdoor Show on Earth," takes over the city in a major way. It's the richest rodeo around, with $2 million in prizes. From morning stampede breakfasts and parades to a roller-coaster midway and live concerts, there is a lot to soak in. Visit www.calgarystampede.com for more information on the event and how to get tickets.

The rodeo at the Calgary Stampede is the most lucrative on the circuit.

Calgary in Two Days

1 Calgary Farmer's Market
2 Heritage Park
3 Calgary Olympic Park
4 Kensington

You've seen all the main highlights of Calgary and its bustling downtown core. A second day will let you branch out to roam the wider regions of Calgary. But you'll need a vehicle for today's trip.

❶ Calgary Farmer's Market. A year-round indoor market has rows and rows of seasonal produce, organic meat, and artwork from more than 100 vendors. *510–77 Ave SE.* ☎ *403/240-9113. Free admission. Thurs–Sun 9am–5pm.*

Continue south on Crowchild Trail, turning east on Glenmore Trail. Turn south on 14th Street SW into the Glenmore Park.

❷ Heritage Park. A re-created pioneer village covers the years from 1860 to 1940. Ride on a steam train or paddlewheeler, or go for a ride on the antique midway. *1900 Heritage Dr. SW.* ☎ *403/268-8500. Adults $25, children 3–17 $19, families $87. May 19–Sept 3 9am–5pm; rest of year Sat–Sun 9am–5pm.*

Head north out of Glenmore Park onto 14th Street SW, turning west or left on Glenmore Trail. Follow until it meets up with the Trans-Canada Hwy. 1. Go west to the next exit.

❸ Calgary Olympic Park. The slopes that hosted luge, bobsled, and ski jumping in the 1988 Olympics have a small ski hill open to all during the winter. In summer, it turns into a playground with mountain biking, zip-lining, and great views from the top of the Ski Jump Tower. There's also an Olympic museum and Canada's Sports Hall of Fame. *88 Canada Olympic Rd. SW.* ☎ *403/247-5452. Free admission; pay per activity. Hours vary.*

Take the Trans-Canada Hwy. 1 east back towards the city. Turn east at Memorial Drive, following the Bow River until you reach Kensington Road.

❹ Kensington. To mix and mingle with Calgarians, head to Kensington Road. There are pubs, cafes, unique boutiques, some excellent restaurants—**Vero Bistro Moderne,** 209 10th St. N (☎ 403/283-8988) has some of the city's best Italian food—and a relaxed feel in one of the city's liveliest neighborhoods.

Calgary Olympic Park offers lots of activities and Canada's Sports Hall of Fame.

The Canadian Rockies

Calgary **Dining & Lodging**

Accommodations

Acclaim Hotel 10
The Fairmont Palliser 7
Holiday Inn Express 14
Hotel Arts 6
Hotel Elan 1
Kensington
Riverside Inn 13

Dining

Bettliner Diner 5
Charbar 9
The Coup 3
Farm 2
Peter's Drive In 11
River Café 12
Teatro 8
UNA Pizza
and Wine 4

Dining & Lodging A to Z

Restaurants

★ **Beltliner Diner** NORTH OF 17TH AVENUE *DINER* There are plenty of places for brunch in Calgary, but this is my current favorite. It's a stylish, modern version of a classic diner, with plenty of old-school entrees like Eggs Bennie and more current options like a lobster mac 'n'cheese and salmon pozole. Come early to beat line-ups. *242 12 Ave SW.* ☎ *587/955-1555. www.thebeltliner.com. Entrees $14–$25. Mon–Sat 7am–10pm, Sun 7am–4pm. Map p 122.*

★★ **Charbar** EAST VILLAGE *STEAKHOUSE* A beautiful old warehouse has been transformed into a hip Argentine-style grill house next to the Bow River. Slow-grilled meats are the stars here. Order a grass-fed Alberta butcher steak, with mint broccoli or roasted beets on the side. There's also a large selection of ceviche, the other house specialty. Or just come for a drink and tapas and enjoy the roof-top patio on a summer evening. *618 Confluence Way SE.* ☎ *403/452-3115. www.charbar.ca. Entrees $17–$49. Mon–Wed 11:30am–10pm, Thurs–Fri 11:30am–12am, Sat 10am–12am, Sun 10am–10pm. Map p 122.*

★ **The Coup** 17TH AVENUE *VEGETARIAN* Healthy, fresh, creative fusion food stars at this hip spot on 17th Avenue. Most ingredients are vegetarian, organic, and local. There are jam-packed salads, falafel quesadillas, and a dragon bowl that has steamed veggies, tofu, and brown rice. There's also a fun cocktail list. *924 17th Ave. SW.* ☎ *403/541-1041. www.thecoup.ca. Entrees $13–$16. AE, MC, V. Tues–Thurs 11:30am–3pm, 5–10pm; Fri 11:30am–3pm, 5–11pm; Sat 9am–3pm, 5–11pm; Sun 9am–3pm, 5–9pm. Map p 122.*

★ **Farm** 17TH AVENUE *REGIONAL* Just as the name suggests, this a place to sample wholesome, simple food. It's classic "slow food" style, but it's more precious than most pastoral country tables. Small plates and platters make sampling from the outstanding cheese selection a good idea. The mac 'n' cheese is the best in town. The ambience is as relaxing as the countryside. *1006 17th Ave. SW.* ☎ *403/245-2276. www.farm-restaurant.com. Entrees $14–$24. AE, MC, V. Daily 11:30am–10pm. Map p 122*

kids Peter's Drive In NORTH OF DOWNTOWN *DINER* If you're en route to Banff from the Calgary airport (or vice versa), drop by this legendary and truly retro (it's been around since 1964) "drive-in" just off the Trans-Canada Highway for

The open-concept kitchen at Farm.

burgers, fries, onion rings, and a shake. You can be served in the car or go through the drive-through window. *219 16th Ave.* ☎ *403/277-2747. www.petersdrivein.com. Entrees $4–$5. No credit cards. Daily 9am–midnight. Map p 122.*

★★ River Café PRINCE'S
ISLAND PARK *REGIONAL* From the picturesque setting in a wooden lodge on an island in the Bow River to a menu that exemplifies regional and seasonal Alberta cuisine, this is a rich experience. Start with the emblematic fish and game platter. Then opt for bison or beef. If you're only in town for 1 night and it's not storming out, then this should be your choice for dinner. *Prince's Island Park.* ☎ *403/261-7670. www.river-cafe.com. Entrees $26–$49. AE, MC, V. Mon–Fri 11am–11pm, Sat–Sun 10am–11pm. Map p 122.*

★★ Teatro DOWNTOWN
EUROPEAN For a refined, romantic meal, come to this dazzling room inside the historic Dominion Bank building. It's mainly Italian food, since the owner is Italian, but there's a delicate high-end French influence. Pastas come with duck Bolognese or Atlantic lobster sauces, for example. Drop in for a

Teatro is located inside the historic Dominion Bank building.

martini or a glass of wine before going to a show, or for a nightcap. *200 8th Ave. SE, Olympic Plaza.* ☎ *403/290-1012. www.teatro.ca. Entrees $24–$49. AE, DC, MC, V. Mon–Fri 11:30am–10pm, Sat–Sun 5–10pm. Map p 122.*

★★ UNA Pizza and Wine 17TH
AVENUE *PIZZA* Great service, fabulously simple Italian food, a casual and bustling atmosphere, NHL hockey players possibly sitting nearby, even a kids' menu—the only problem at UNA is that you can't make reservations. Come before 6pm or after 7:30pm, or be prepared to stroll 17th Ave while you wait. *618 17th Ave. SW.* ☎ *403/453-1183. www.unapizzeria.com. Entrees $15–$19. Daily 11:30am–1am. Map p 122.*

Accommodations
Acclaim Hotel AIRPORT If all you need is a good bed before or after your flight, this stylish airport hotel is a great choice. Complimentary shuttle, big fluffy beds, a rooftop hot tub, and a fitness club will ease your travel-weary bones. It's way out of town, though. *123 Freeport Blvd. NE.* ☎ *866/955-0008 or 403/291-8000. www.acclaimhotel.ca. 123 units. Doubles $150–$325. AE, MC, V. Map p 122.*

★ The Fairmont Palliser
DOWNTOWN Opened in 1914, this historic landmark has deep roots in the Calgary community. Rooms here are notoriously cramped, as in most urban hotels of this vintage, but they retain an old-world elegance typical of Fairmont. The Fairmont Gold rooms have extra value with a private concierge, private check-in, and separate dining area. The lobby could use some freshening up. *133 9th Ave. SW.* ☎ *800/441-1414 or 403/262-1234. www.fairmont.com. 407 units. Doubles $149–$549. AE, DC, MC, V. Map p 122.*

A stately guest room at the Fairmont Palliser Hotel.

kids Holiday Inn Express

DOWNTOWN   My choice for best mid-range hotel in town, this includes the predictable high-rise hotel experience found in many hotels, plus breakfast. The rooms are average and the location good. There's a small fitness center. Kids eat free in the grill next door. *1020 8th Ave. ☎ 877/660-8550 or 403/ 269-8262. www.hiexpress.com. 56 units. Doubles $198–$252. AE, MC, DC, V. Map p 122.*

Hotel Arts STAMPEDE GROUNDS

Hipsters gather at this design-forward hotel that's steps from trendy bars and restaurants, and also happens to be just a few blocks from the Stampede Grounds, the Saddledome, and the Calgary Tower. Rooms are updated, chic versions of a Holiday Inn. Don't expect anything special from them. But the common areas are oozing with pizzazz. *119 12 Ave. SW. ☎ 403/266-4611. www.hotelarts.ca. 185 rooms. Doubles $179–$369. AE, MC, V. Map p 122.*

Hotel Elan 17TH AVENUE   For

longer stays or families wanting more space, the suites at the Euro-styled hotel will be very comfortable. It's also a block from the bustling shops of 17th Ave. Breakfast is included. *1122 16th Ave. SW. ☎ 403/229-2040. www.hotelelan.ca. 62 rooms. Doubles from $249, suites from $309. AE, MC, V, DC. Map p 122.*

★★ Kensington Riverside Inn

KENSINGTON   This boutique inn—on the north side of the river a short walk from downtown—is private, expensive, design-forward, and chic. The rooms are large, the ambiance cool, and the restaurant possibly the best in town. *1126 Memorial Dr. NW. ☎ 877/313-3733 or 403/ 228-4442. www.kensingtonriverside inn.com. 19 units. Doubles $299–$399. AE, DC, MC, V. Map p 122.*

The stylish Kensington Riverside Inn.

Alberta Rockies **Dining & Lodging**

Dining
Bears Paw Bakery **3**
Earl's **2**
Fiddle River **10**
Jasper Brewing
   Company **11**
Moose's Nook
   Northern Grill **5**
North Face Pizza **9**
Syrahs of Jasper **7**
Tekarra Lodge **12**

Lodging
Alpine Village **13**
Fairmont Jasper
   Park Lodge **6**
Jasper International
   Hostel **14**
Mount Edith Cavell Hostel **17**
Park Place Inn **11**
Pine Bungalows **12**
Pyramid Lake Resort **1**
Wapiti Campground **16**
Whistlers Campground **15**

0   1/4 mi
0   1/4 km

△ Campground
✚ Hospital/First Aid
P Parking

Jasper

Pyramid Lake Rd.
Elm
Hazel Ave.
Geikie
Patricia
Connaught Dr.
16
Athabasca River
93A
Miette River
93
To Banff

Canmore

0   1/4 mi
0   1/4 km

17th St.
17th St.
15th St.
14th St.
13th St.
11th St.
Fairholme Dr.
8th Ave.
7th Ave.
10th St.
9th St.
8th St.   Main St.
7th St.
6th St.
5th St.
4th St.
River Rd.
8th Ave.
7th Ave.
Railway Ave.
2th Ave.
1st Ave.
1A
Hospital Pl.
Trans-Canada Highway
Palliser Trail
Benchlands Trail
Policeman's Creek
Kananaskis Way
Montane Rd.
1A
Bow River

✚ Hospital
P Parking
••• Walking Path

Dining
Communitea Café **2**
Crazyweed Kitchen **1**
Rocky Mountain
   Flatbread Company **4**
The Trough Dining Company **3**

Lodging
Alpine Club of
   Canada Clubhouse **8**
Blackstone Mountain Lodge **6**
Delta Lodge at Kananaskis **7**
Paintbox Lodge **5**

Dining & Lodging A to Z

Bear's Paw Bakery.

Restaurants
Bear's Paw Bakery JASPER *BAKERY/CAFE* With two locations, this bakery is very popular. There are fresh sandwiches, granola to go, superb fruit tarts, and a huge variety of cookies, bars, and yummy delights—including dog treats. Their freshly baked bread is served at nearly every restaurant in town. *610 Connaught Dr. and 4 Cedar Ave.* ☎ *780/852-3233. www.bearspaw bakery.com. Sandwiches $7–$12. AE, MC, V. Daily 7am–6pm. Map p 126.*

★★ Communitea Café
CANMORE *CAFE/VEGETARIAN* Choose from more than 80 blends of loose-leaf tea at this funky hangout. Breakfasts and lunches are healthy, affordable, and tasty. Build your own rice bowl with organic brown rice, steamed veggies, and flavorful Asian sauces. There are also great snacks like sushi, shrimp rolls, organic eda-mame—and quite possibly the best lattes in town, brewed in a one-of-a-kind espresso machine. This is a place with heart. *117–1001 6th Ave., corner of 10th St.* ☎ *403/678-6818. www.thecommunitea.com. Entrees $8–$14. MC, V. Mon–Fri 9am–4pm, Sat–Sun 9am–5pm. Map p 126.*

★ Crazyweed Kitchen
CAN-MORE *GLOBAL/FUSION* Slightly

A bustling night at Crazyweed Kitchen.

unpredictable and always provocative, Crazyweed's is both chaotic and creative. The food here could just be the most incredible of your life, particularly the kashmiri lamb balls and the Thai grilled chicken. But service is erratic, either pompously absent or delightfully charming. *1600 Railway Ave.* ☎ *403/609-2530. www.crazyweed.ca. Entrees $21–$38. AE, MC, V. Daily 11:30am–3pm; Mon–Thurs, Sun 5–10pm; Fri–Sat 5–10pm. Map p 126.*

Earl's JASPER *CANADIAN* A real crowd-pleaser, Earl's is a good choice for just about anybody—families, couples, or friends. Part of a popular Western Canada chain, there's a bit of Mexican, Asian, and European served here, from burgers to Thai curries to brick-oven pizzas. They also have the nicest outdoor patio in town, including heaters on a chilly evening. *600 Patricia St., upstairs.* ☎ *780/852-2393. www.earls.ca. Reservations recommended in summer. Entrees $16–$32. AE, MC, V. Daily 11:30am–midnight. Map p 126.*

Fiddle River JASPER *CANADIAN* Upstairs, above Connaught Street, there's an ever-changing menu here

that almost always has Canadiana favorites like Alberta-raised beef, caribou meatloaf, and a steaming bison stew, as well as pumpkin-seed trout and a seafood kettle. The service is casual and friendly, and the views are divine. *620 Connaught St., upstairs.* ☎ *780/852-3032. www.fiddleriverrestaurant.com. Entrees $22–$39. AE, MC, V. Daily 5pm–midnight. Map p 126.*

Jasper Brewing Company JASPER *BREWPUB* A warm and cozy place for a pint and a burger, the bartender will suggest the fish and chips or sirloin steak burger. There are big-screen TVs and a cozy fireplace. Highly regarded ales, pilsners, and stouts are brewed in the back; a sample of six costs $15. *624 Connaught Dr.* ☎ *780/852-4111. www.jasperbrewingco.com. Entrees $11–$26. AE, MC, V. Daily 11:30am–1am. Map p 126.*

★★ **Moose's Nook Northern Grill** JASPER *REGIONAL* The best meal in Jasper is to be had at the Jasper Park Lodge's recently revamped steakhouse. Choose from beef, bison, elk or lamb steaks, then add on the side dishes and a salad. The wine list features

A dish from the Moose's Nook Northern Grill inside the Fairmont Jasper Park Lodge.

A kid-sized flatbread pizza from the Rocky Mountain Flatbread Company.

surprisingly good Canadian labels—ask for guidance. The only thing lacking is a good view. Open summers only. *In the Fairmont Jasper Park Lodge, Old Lodge Rd.* ☎ *780/852-6052. www.fairmont. com/jasper. Entrees $35–$55. AE, DC, MC, V. Daily 6–9pm. Map p 126.*

North Face Pizza JASPER *PIZZA* If you want to order in, do so from Jasper's best pizza joint. Free delivery anywhere in town. There are also burgers, salads, pastas, sandwiches, and wings on offer, plus locally brewed beer from Big Rock Brewery on tap. Eat in (order at the counter) if you want to mingle with the local under-30 crowd. *618 Connaught Dr.* ☎ *780/852-5830. Pizzas $12–$22. AE, MC, V. Daily 11am–2am. Map p 126.*

kids Rocky Mountain Flatbread Company CANMORE *MEDITERRANEAN* The wood-fired clay oven here is reportedly the largest in Canada. Handcrafted flatbread pizzas are made with organic flour, regional cheeses, and fresh, creative toppings. The Nemo has prawns, artichokes, and asiago cheese. Salads are big and creative. Pint-sized portions for kids and a kid-friendly play area, where they can bake their own pretend pizzas, are available. *838 10th St.* ☎ *403/ 609-5508. www.rockymountainflat bread.ca. Entrees $14–$28. AE, MC, V. Daily 11:30am–10pm. Map p 126.*

★ **Syrahs of Jasper** JASPER *EUROPEAN* It's the consistency, with quality food and good service, that keeps this spot a top choice in Jasper. The best dishes are traditional Swiss blended with tastes from around the world, like veal eminence Zurich-style and filet mignon with pesto and goat cheese. Portions are very large. There's an accessible wine list. *606 Patricia St.* ☎ *780/852-4559. www. syrahsofjasper.com. Reservations recommended. Entrees $17–$49. AE, MC, V. Daily 5–10pm. Map p 126.*

★★ **Tekarra Restaurant** JASPER *INTERNATIONAL* This little cabin inside the sprawling lodge of the same name draws Jasper's keenest foodies. The menu spans from locally sourced ingredients like bison and Alberta beef to venison and Arctic char, always with a creative flair that's both rustic and refined. All the smoking, curing, and baking is done in house. Open only from late May to early October. *In Tekarra Lodge, Hwy. 93A 1 km (.6 mile) south of Jasper Townsite.* ☎ *780/852-4624. www.tekarra restaurant.com. Reservations recommended. Entrees $26–$42. MC, V. Daily 5:30–10pm. Map p. 126.*

★ **The Trough Dining Co.** CANMORE *BISTRO* With a relaxed and intimate vibe, this is Canmore's

One of the rustic cottages at Alpine Village.

top restaurant. Flavors are powerful and intense in every dish. Labor-intensive entrees include jerk-spiced Alberta baby back ribs and scallops with pork belly, both chock full of fresh ingredients and surprising tastes. Staff is highly professional and the wine list is extensive. If you're on a budget, come for just a glass of wine and dessert. *725 9th St., behind Main St. btw. 6th and 7th*

aves. ☎ 403/678-2820. www.the trough.ca. Reservations highly recommended. Entrees $35–$42. AE, MC, V. Wed–Mon 5:30–10pm. Map p 126.

Accommodations

Alpine Club of Canada Clubhouse CANMORE   The national headquarters for Canada's Alpine Club is just outside Canmore and houses a sweet hostel-style inn. It's a budget-friendly choice and a hub for meeting fellow hikers, skiers and adventurers. There's a kitchen, barbecues, laundry and a great view. *201 Indian Flats Rd.* ☎ *403/678-3200. www.alpineclubofcanada.ca. 12 units. $30 for club members, $41 for nonmembers. MC, V. Map p 126.*

★★ **Alpine Village** JASPER   On the banks of the rushing Athabasca River, these rustic yet stylish log cottages make a cozy, romantic base, good for simply enjoying the natural beauty of the park. They range from brand-new deluxe bedroom suites to quaint cabins dating back to 1941. All have some form of

The urban decor at Blackstone Mountain Lodge.

A public area inside the historic Fairmont Jasper Park Lodge.

a kitchenette. Cabins farthest from the road are quieter, but those along the river (next to the road) have the best views. *2.5km (1½ miles) south of Jasper Townsite on the Icefields Pkwy., Hwy. 93, at the junction with Hwy. 93A.* ☎ *780/852-3285. www.alpinevillagejasper.com. 41 units, 28 with kitchenettes. Cabins $210–$510. MC, V. Closed mid-Oct to Apr. Map p 126.*

Blackstone Mountain Lodge

CANMORE   Settle into your own condo at this vacation rental property. The decor is urban chic, but the views are definitely all natural. Fully equipped units have one, two, or three bedrooms, private balconies, granite countertops, stainless steel appliances, and even a wine cabinet. A good base if you're coming for a week or more. *170 Kananaskis Way.* ☎ *888/830-8883 or 403/609-8098. www.blackstone canmore.ca. 123 units. Doubles from $280, 2-bedroom suites from $459. AE, MC, V. Map p 126.*

★★★ Fairmont Jasper Park Lodge

Built in 1923, this historic lodge epitomizes the pampered wilderness experience. It's like an upscale summer camp for adults spread over the largest commercial property in the Canadian Rockies (with a revered golf course, gorgeous lake, stables, and outdoor pool). The guest rooms are mostly in single-story cabins and cottages spread throughout the property. A new spa opened in late 2010. Ask about packages and promotions. *4km (2½ miles) east of Jasper on Hwy. 16, 3.2km (2 miles) southeast off Maligne Lake Rd.* ☎ *800/441-1414 or 780/852-3301. www.fairmont.com/jasper. 446 units. Doubles $229–$609. AE, DC, MC, V. Map p 126.*

The cozy Paintbox Lodge.

south from the townsite to Cavell Rd.; turn west and continue for 13km (8 miles) to the hostel, on the east side of the road. ☎ 866/762-4122 or 780/852-3215. www.hihostels.ca. 32 beds. Shared dorm $27. MC, V. Map p 126.

★★ Paintbox Lodge CANMORE

A winner for its cozy vibe, friendly service, and location (just steps from Main St.), this is Canmore's best boutique-style inn. The eight guest rooms are all different and all comfortable; upstairs ones have high ceilings with a cozy sitting area. The two-bedroom suite is good for families. 629 10th St. ☎ 888/678-6100 or 403/609-0482. www.paintboxlodge.com. 5 units. Doubles $210–$279. AE, MC, V. Map p 126.

★★ Park Place Inn JASPER

This is the only place in town one could call an upscale boutique inn, with reasonable rates to boot. The 12 spacious rooms have a cowboy heritage theme, with beautiful linens, goose-down duvets, hardwood floors, huge tubs (many are claw-foot style), and plenty of space. Located upstairs on the bustling Patricia Street, it feels downtown (if that's possible in Jasper). 623 Patricia St. ☎ 866/852-9770 or 780/852-9770. www.park placeinn.com. 14 rooms. Doubles $229–$269. AE, MC, V. Map p 126.

Jasper International Hostel

JASPER   This is the best choice for budget travelers in Jasper, but it's best if you have a car. There are two dorms that are very big, where you'll sleep in bunk beds. Bathrooms are all shared. Family rooms are also available. The shared kitchen is very handy. There is a fun full-time activity program that will get you out exploring Jasper. 4km (2½ miles) south of Jasper Townsite on Hwy. 93, turn west on Tramway Rd. and follow for 3km (1¾ miles). ☎ 877/852-0781 or 780/852-3215. www.hihostels.ca. 5 units (2 dormitory-style rooms and 3 private family rooms), 84 beds total. Private doubles $81; dorm beds $32. MC, V. Map p 126.

Mt. Edith Cavell Hostel JASPER

This simple and remote shelter is a good base for backpackers and hikers. It sleeps 32 people in two cabins. It also has no electricity or flush toilets, but there's a self-catering kitchen and awe-inspiring scenery all around. Private doubles are available. Members of Hostelling International receive a discount. Open mid-June to mid-October only. On Cavell Rd.; take Hwy. 93A

Pine Bungalows JASPER   Cabins ensconced along the Athabasca River are nostalgic and family-friendly. Most of them have fireplaces, and nearly all of them have kitchenettes. The best cabins are nos. 1 through 12, right on the river. A good choice if you don't need to be pampered and want your

A tent site at Whistlers Campground.

privacy. There's a 2-night minimum. Open May through early October. *Just off Hwy. 16 and the Jasper Townsite turnoff.* ☎ *780/852-3491. www.pinebungalows.com. 72 cabins, 57 with kitchens and 25 motel rooms. Cabins $160–$220. AE, MC, V. Map p 126.*

Pyramid Lake Resort JASPER With a picturesque lakeside setting, this small resort offers plenty of activities, solitude, and lovely new rooms. Walls are thin. The top-floor Cavell Rooms, built in the late 1990s, are the largest and most modern guest rooms, perfect for families planning on staying a few days. It's slow-paced up here and you'll need a car. *6km (3¾ miles) north from Jasper Townsite on Pyramid Lake Rd.* ☎ *888/852-7737 or 780/852-4900. www.mpljasper.com. 62 units. Doubles $262–$292. AE, DC, MC, V. Map p 126.*

Wapiti Campground JASPER This is the only campground in the park that's open year-round, and in summer it's quieter than Whistlers. There are 362 sites, 322 of which are for tents only. More than a third of the sites remain accessible in

winter. There are often elk roaming about here—remember to keep your distance. *4km (2½ miles) south of Jasper Townsite on the Icefields Pkwy., Hwy. 93, on the east side. Summer: 362 sites, 40 with electrical hookup. $27 tents; $32 RVs. Open Victoria Day long weekend (late May) and mid-June to early Sept. Winter: 93 sites, 40 with electrical hookup. $18 tents; $22 RVs. Early Oct to early May. Map p 126.*

Whistlers Campground JASPER This is the biggest campground in Jasper, with 781 sites. It's also just south of town, on the Icefields Parkway (Hwy. 93). It can feel busy and noisy. There are fun interpretive programs put on in the summer evenings. Of the 177 RV sites, 100 have electrical hookups only; the other 77 sites have full hookups. I've twice seen a bear here—so keep your food stored properly. *3km (1¾ miles) south of Jasper Townsite on the Icefields Pkwy., Hwy. 93, on the west side. 781 sites, 100 with electrical hookup only, 77 with full hookup. $23–$27 tents; $32 electrical hookup; $38 full hookup. Early May to early Oct. Map p 126.*

BC Rockies **Dining & Lodging**

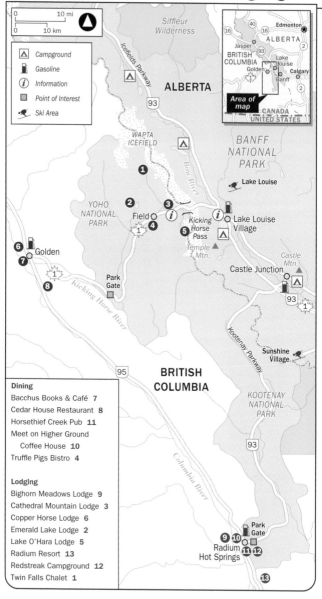

0 | 10 mi
0 | 10 km

- ▲ Campground
- ⬛ Gasoline
- ⓘ Information
- ⬛ Point of Interest
- ⛷ Ski Area

Siffleur
Wilderness

ALBERTA

93

WAPTA
ICEFIELD

BANFF
NATIONAL
PARK

Bow River

Lake Louise

YOHO
NATIONAL
PARK

Field

Kicking
Horse
Pass

Lake Louise
Village

Temple
Mtn.

Castle
Mtn.

Castle Junction

93

1

Golden

Kicking Horse River

Park
Gate

Kootenay Parkway

Sunshine
Village

BRITISH
COLUMBIA

95

KOOTENAY
NATIONAL
PARK

93

Columbia River

Park
Gate

Radium
Hot Springs

16 · 40 · Edmonton
ALBERTA
Jasper · 93
Lake
Louise
BRITISH
COLUMBIA
Golden · Banff · Calgary
2
Area
of
map
CANADA
UNITED STATES

Dining

Bacchus Books & Café **7**
Cedar House Restaurant **8**
Horsethief Creek Pub **11**
Meet on Higher Ground
  Coffee House **10**
Truffle Pigs Bistro **4**

Lodging

Bighorn Meadows Lodge **9**
Cathedral Mountain Lodge **3**
Copper Horse Lodge **6**
Emerald Lake Lodge **2**
Lake O'Hara Lodge **5**
Radium Resort **13**
Redstreak Campground **12**
Twin Falls Chalet **1**

Dining & Lodging A to Z

Restaurants

Bacchus Books & Café GOLDEN *CAFE* A range of sandwiches (from seafood club to roasted veggie panini), daily homemade soups and specials and loads of baked goods make this a cozy, friendly spot in the heart of Golden. *409 9th Ave N.* ☎ *250/344-5600. www. bacchusbooks.ca Lunch $7–$12. AE, MC, V. Mon–Sat 9am–5:30pm, Sun 10am–4pm. Map p 134.*

★★ Cedar House Restaurant

GOLDEN *CANADIAN* Fresh and inspired food in a rural setting, the passionate chefs here offer simple and local ingredients, creating entrees like tamarind free-range chicken breast, slow-braised lamb shank, and a spectacular espresso and maple syrup buffalo steak. Meats are all natural, and the fish is wild. For dessert, there are homemade sorbets. *735 Hefti Rd.* ☎ *250/ 344-4679. www.cedarhousechalets. com. Entrees $29–$39. MC, V. Reservations required. Wed–Sun 5–9pm. Map p 134.*

Horsethief Creek Pub RADIUM *PUB* The menu here is almost as expansive as the views across the Columbia Valley. The famous half-pound burger comes with mushrooms, bacon, and melted cheese. Pasta lovers will be tempted by Kootenai curry fettuccini or Louisiana prawn penne. It's also a nice spot for an afternoon beer and nibbles. *7538 Main St.* ☎ *250/347-6400. www. horsethiefpub.ca. Entrees $15–$29. MC, V. Summer daily noon–10pm; winter closed Mon–Tues. Pub open weekends until midnight. Map p 134.*

Meet on Higher Ground Coffee House RADIUM *CAFE* The options in Radium aren't great, but this cozy cafe has by far the best coffee and baked goods in the village. Breakfast bagels and hearty sandwiches make for good picnics. *7527 Main St., Ste. 6.* ☎ *250/347-6567. www.meetonhigherground.ca. Breakfasts and sandwiches $7–$12. MC, V. Daily 6am–5pm. Map p 134.*

★★ Truffle Pigs Bistro FIELD

CAFE Field took center stage for

A burger from the Horsethief Creek Pub.

Field's Truffle Pigs Bistro.

foodies when this cafe became a bistro and moved across the street. The chef offers options like coconut curry ragout and an unforgettable lamb and fig sandwich. Handmade desserts and a good wine list make it the best stop between Lake Louise and Golden. *100 Centre St. ☎ 250/343-6303. www.trufflepigs. com. Lunch $9–$21; dinner entrees $18–$36. MC, V. Summer daily 7–10:30am; winter 11am–9pm. Map p 134.*

Cathedral Mountain Lodge's "Grand Room."

Accommodations
Bighorn Meadows Lodge

RADIUM   At last something besides a motel in Radium. These are vacation rentals at a condo development on the west side of town. They're quite new, so they're clean and have great views. Units have private balconies with barbecues overlooking the golf course. Guest rooms are a bargain but don't have kitchens. *10 Bighorn Blvd., Radium Hot Springs, BC. ☎ 877/344-2323 or 250/347-2323. www.bighornmeadows.ca. 96 units. Apartments $139–$319. AE, MC, V. Map p 134.*

★★ Cathedral Mountain
Lodge FIELD   If it's a cozy log cabin in a peaceful and powerful setting you're after, this is an excellent choice. This lodge offers a beautiful blend of privacy and luxury tucked beneath its namesake mountain along the banks of the glacier-fed Kicking Horse River. Quintessential cabins are functional and cute (if somewhat close together), with fireplaces, modern bathtubs, and fluffy duvets. *Take the Trans-Canada Hwy. 5km (3 miles) west from the Alberta–British Columbia border or 2km (1¼ miles) east of*

Field, BC and turn northwest on Yoho Valley Rd.; continue 4km (2½ miles) to lodge. ☎ 866/619-6442 or 250/343-6442. www.cathedral mountainlodge.com. 31 units. Cabins $279–$529. AE, MC, V. Map p 134.

Copper Horse Lodge

GOLDEN At the base of Kicking Horse Mountain Resort, this boutique-sized inn has a stylish mountain vibe, lovely service, and a supremely relaxing feel. Built only a few years ago, it's a good choice if your aim is to rip it up at the resort or find some quiet romance. Otherwise, it's out of the way. At end of Kicking Horse Mountain. Rd.; turn right after the gondolas. ☎ 877/544-7644 or 250/344-7644. www.copper horselodge.com. 10 units. Doubles $235–$285. MC, V. Map p 134.

★ Emerald Lake Lodge

FIELD This luxurious but cozy lodge, made up of 24 buildings on a 5-hectare (12 acres) peninsula in the heart of Yoho National Park is splendid. Each guest room has a fieldstone fireplace and warm, rustic decor, including dark green marble vanities in many bathrooms (although others remain in need of a facelift). Most rooms have a balcony. The real star, however, is Emerald Lake itself, a glow of turquoise that never escapes the corner of your eye. 1 Emerald Lake Rd., Field, BC. Take Trans-Canada Hwy. 2km (1¼ miles) south of Field to Emerald Lake Rd. turnoff; continue 8km (5 miles). ☎ 800/663-6336 or 250/343-6321. www.crmr.com. 85 units. Doubles $329–$419. AE, MC, V. Map p 134.

★★★ Lake O'Hara Lodge

YOHO NATIONAL PARK In a secluded alpine valley, there are no phones, no television, no roads, and no cars here (see the box "Lake O'Hara: Getting to Paradise," p 108). This is a paradise that is one of a kind. Cabins have comfortable beds and modern bathrooms; meals are included. It's a wonderful getaway for city slickers and a true mecca for mountain lovers of all ages. Reserve well in advance. Access via the Parks Canada bus that leaves the Lake O'Hara parking lot. June–Sept ☎ 250/343-6418, Oct–May ☎ is 403/678-4110. www.lakeohara.com. 8 lodge rooms,

A room inside the Copper Horse Lodge.

A room inside the Emerald Lake Lodge.

8 cabins. Rates include all meals, tips, taxes, and bus transportation. Doubles $665–$945, all meals included. No credit cards. Map p 134.

Redstreak Campground

RADIUM HOT SPRINGS There's lots to do at Parks Canada's largest campground in Kootenay National Park, including nightly entertainment in the summer and a network of trails heading into the park. It's located behind the Visitors Centre. Reserve a campsite online at www. pccamping.ca or call

One of the cabins at Lake O'Hara Lodge.

☎ 877/737-3783. *2.5km (1½ miles) southwest of Radium Hot Springs, turn east off Hwy. 93 at the sign.* ☎ *250/347-9505. 242 sites, 38 with electrical hookup only, 50 with full hookup. $27–$38. AE, MC, V. May 11–Oct 8. Map p 134.*

Truffle Pigs Lodge FIELD

This cozy and simple lodge located in the heart of the sweet little village of Field is a good choice. Rooms are quite basic, but the friendly vibes, great views and good restaurant more than make up for that. There's a family suite for up to six. *100 Centre St., Field.* ☎ *250/343-6303. www.trufflepigs.com. 13 rooms $175–$225. Map p 134.*

Twin Falls Chalet YOHO

NATIONAL PARK Tucked beneath one of the loveliest waterfalls in Yoho (and the competition is fierce!), this historic log cabin was built in 1908 and offers simple, rustic backcountry lodging for hikers. There is no electricity, although solar panels keep things warm and bright. *In Yoho Valley. Reserve by telephone only at* ☎ *403/228-7079. www.twinfallschalet.ca. 15 beds. $250 per person, 2-night minimum, includes all meals. No credit cards. Late June to mid-Sept. Map p 134.* ●

6 The Great Outdoors

The Best **Hiking in Banff**

Previous Page: Canoeing on the Bow River.

1 Cascade Ampitheatre
2 C-Level Cirque
3 Sundance Canyon
4 Castle Lookout
5 Cory Pass
6 Ink Pots
7 Sunshine Meadows
8 Lake Agnes/Beehives
9 Lakeshore Trail
10 Moraine Lakeshore Trail
11 Paradise Valley/Larch Valley
12 Plain of the Six Glaciers
13 Saddleback Pass
14 Bow Glacier Falls
15 Helen Lake
16 Nigel Pass
17 Parker Ridge
18 Peyto Lake/Bow Summit
19 Wilcox Pass

10 mi
10 km

The hiking season in Banff usually gets started in mid-June and winds down in October. Trails on the southern slopes and at lower elevations are free of snow earlier in the season and open earlier. In spring, trails are often extremely wet and muddy. In autumn many days are sunny and warm, but the variability of the weather poses a new challenge, since snow may begin to accumulate over high passes.

Town of Banff Hikes

★ **Cascade Amphitheater.** You can't miss Cascade Mountain—the beautiful pyramid-shaped peak at the northeastern end of Banff Avenue. One of the most rewarding day hikes in the townsite area, this is a demanding outing that starts (and later finishes) at the Mt. Norquay day lodge, and takes you into a high alpine cirque in a hanging valley with a lush carpet of subalpine wildflowers. The trail crests at a dramatic point on the south edge of the meadows, on a small knoll of rockslide debris. *7.7km (4.8 miles) each way. Strenuous. Elevation gain is 640m (2,100 ft.). 6 hr. round-trip. Trail head is Mt. Norquay ski area. Map p 140.*

★ **C-Level Cirque.** This trail has wonderful panoramic views and is a great afternoon getaway from busy Banff Avenue. After alighting on a stunning view of Lake Minnewanka, the trail heads back into the now-subalpine forest before ending in a small cirque (like a bowl with a circular ridge surrounding it) at the highest part of the valley. Look for calypso orchids, marmots, and pika as you climb to the treeless alpine zone. *3.9km (2.4 miles) each way. Moderate. Elevation gain 455m (1,493 ft.). 3 hr. round-trip. Trail head is Upper Bankhead picnic area parking lot, 3.5km (2.3 miles) on Minnewanka Rd. from the Minnewanka interchange on the Trans-Canada Hwy. Map p 140.*

kids **Sundance Canyon.** A gentle hike that leaves from the Cave and Basin Historic Site is good in spring and fall. There are nice views of the Sawback Range and the pinnacle of Mt. Edith. It goes up a paved trail, turning at Sundance Creek and continuing on to an extraordinary canyon with giant boulders. Head over the bridge and up the stairs for the best views. *4.3km (2.7 miles) each way. Easy. Elevation gain 143m (469 ft.). 3 hr. round-trip. Trail head at Cave and Basin Historic Site. Map p 140.*

Bow Valley Parkway & Sunshine Meadows

Castle Lookout. This hike gets you close to a former fire lookout on this scenic mountain. Short but steep, the trail offers an amazing panorama of the glacier-chiseled Bow Valley and Storm Mountain, which is often surrounded by its own gnarly weather system. This trail can be very warm on a sunny day and is

A hiker at Cory Pass.

Easy to Hard: Difficulty Ratings

Hiking times depend on a hiker's experience and fitness, as well as the weather conditions. Hikers of an average fitness level can usually hike 2.5 to 3.5km (1.6–2.2 miles) in an hour. Steeper trails will take longer, and you'll want to add in time for lunch, snack, and rest breaks.

Easy Hikes that are generally smooth and gentle, usually less than 6km (3.7 miles) long with an elevation gain of no more than 300m (984 ft.).

Moderate Hikes up to 13km (8 miles) long on well-established trails with some exposure. Elevation gain can be up to 600m (1,969 ft.).

Difficult Hikes longer than 13km (8 miles), with an elevation gain of more than 600m (1,969 ft.). Often on poorly defined trails, with obstacles and exposed terrain.

Lengths listed here are total distance from the start to the finish of the hikes. Elevation gain is the total ascent from the lowest point on the trail to the highest point.

a great "shoulder season" choice. *3.7km (2.3 miles) each way. Strenuous. Elevation gain 520m (1,706 ft.). 3–4 hr. round-trip. Trail head is parking lot on the north side of the Bow Valley Pkwy. 1A, 5km (3 miles) west of Castle Junction. Map p 140.*

★ **Cory Pass.** This is one of the most strenuous and challenging hikes in Banff, but it's also by far the most spectacular one near the Town of Banff. The highlight is the 2,300m (7,546-ft.) monolithic limestone cliffs of the Sawback Range. The trail starts in a high, subalpine valley bottom and ends in a high alpine zone well above the tree line—tremendous ecological diversity. Be sure to take a good map with you on this trail (see sidebar on p 145). *5.8km (3.6 miles) each way. Very strenuous. Elevation gain is 915m (3,002 ft.). 6–7 hr. round-trip. Trail head is Fireside Picnic Area at the eastern end of the Bow Valley Pkwy. 1A. Map p 140.*

Ink Pots. Continue past the crowds at Johnston Canyon, passing the Upper Falls, twice the size of the lower ones. The trail opens into a lovely, wide valley and takes you to jade-colored natural springs. It's a magical place and very quiet after the rush of the canyon. *5.5km (3.4 miles) each way. Moderate. Elevation gain 243m (797 ft.). 4–5 hr. round-trip. Trail head is Johnston Canyon parking lot, 18km (11 miles) west of Banff on the Bow Valley Pkwy. 1A. Map p 140.*

★★ kids **Sunshine Meadows.** Located high in an alpine bowl that is also the site of the Sunshine Village ski resort in winter, this alpine meadow is famous for its annual display of beautiful wildflowers, and is incredibly easy to get to—just take a shuttle to the Sunshine Village day lodge, where all trail heads are located. **White Mountain Adventures** (☎ 800/408-0005 or 403/762-7889; www.sunshinemeadowsbanff.com) runs a shuttle service to the area.

You'll find beautiful alpine views at Sunshine Meadows.

The Rock Isle Lake trail leads you to the other side of the Continental Divide, into British Columbia's Mt. Assiniboine Provincial Park. Rock Lake is particularly lovely in the calm early morning, when it mirrors the surrounding scenery, and the view stretches off into British Columbia's mountains. It's a favorite of artists and photographers.

The Simpson Pass/Healy Meadows trail is worth an afternoon outing for rewarding views of Wawa Ridge, Mt. Assiniboine, and the Monarch, a massive pyramid-shaped peak. It's a wildflower lover's dream, and a favorite of Banff's old outfitters and pioneers, including Jim Brewster and "Wild Bill" Peyto, two of Banff's original mountain guides. *Rock Isle Lake Trail: 2.5km (1.6 miles) each way. Easy. Elevation gain is 105m (344 ft.). 2 hr. round-trip. Simpson Pass/Healy Meadows: 7.6km (4.7 miles) each way. Moderate. Elevation gain is 160m (525 ft.). 5 hr. round-trip. Map p 140.*

Lake Louise Hikes

★★ **Lake Agnes/Beehives.** In a picturesque hanging valley above Lake Louise, Lake Agnes has been a favorite for more than a century. There are great views of the Bow Valley and wonderful history to be had at the Lake Agnes Teahouse on the shore of the lake, which serves freshly baked scones and tea throughout the summer. From the teahouse, take the trail to the north shore of the lake to connect with the Big Beehive. *5.1km (3.2 miles) each way. Moderate. Elevation gain is 400m (1,312 ft.). 4 hr. round-trip. Trail head is Lake Louise shoreline trail, in front of the Fairmont Chateau Lake Louise. Map p 140.*

kids Lakeshore Trail. This broad, flat trail may be among the most well-trodden paths in Banff National Park. It leads you away from the crowds, around the north shore of the lake to the base of Mt. Victoria and the shimmering Victoria Glacier. There are many benches along

The Lake Agnes Teahouse.

Hiking To-Do List

1. **Select a trail.** Read through the hikes listed here, pick up a map and other hiking guides, and chat with the staff at the Banff Information Centre (224 Banff Ave.; ☎ 403/763-1550; www.pc.gc.ca/banff) or the Lake Louise Visitors Centre (Samson Mall, 101 Lake Louise Dr.; ☎ 403/522-3833) to get the right trail for you.
2. **Get a map.** The best are topographic maps, with a scale of 1:50,000. The Canadian government produces maps with lots of detail, but they are short on hiking trails. GemTrek Maps produces the best hiking maps in the Canadian Rockies. Pick one up in Banff or order at www.gemtrek.com. They're waterproof, tear-resistant, and have topographic contours, key for measuring elevation changes.
3. **Check the weather.** Get the up-to-date forecast by calling Banff National Park (☎ 403/762-1550) or Environment Canada in Banff at ☎ 403/762-2088.
4. **Check trail conditions.** Call the Park at ☎ 403/762-1550 for the latest trail reports, which are also posted around town and online at www.pc.gc.ca/banff. And be sure to find out about any bear warnings and area closures due to bear activity.
5. **Bring plenty of water.** At least 1 liter (2 pints) of water per person, more if you're going on a strenuous full-day hike.
6. **Go in a group.** Some areas of Banff are under bear warnings and hikers must stay in groups of four or six at a time. It's safer, and often more fun!
7. **Tell someone about it.** Let someone know where you're going and when you'll be back.

the trail where you can sit and marvel at Lake Louise's color and beauty. Come early in the morning to beat the crowds. *1.9km (1.2 miles) each way. Easy. No elevation gain. 1 hr. round-trip. Trail head is in front of Fairmont Chateau Lake Louise. Map p 140.*

Moraine Lakeshore Trail.
Moraine Lake is a popular destination, but luckily this trail, along the western shore of the lake, is still a peaceful and pleasant way to enjoy the dramatic and imposing Valley of the Ten Peaks. The best views are at the start of the trail, but for a spectacular view of Moraine Lake at the end of the hike head 5 minutes up to the Moraine Lake Viewpoint, at the south end of the parking lot, following the sign to Consolation Lakes. *1.2km (.7 mile) each way. Easy. No elevation gain. 1 hr. round-trip. Trail head is Moraine Lake parking lot. Map p 140.*

★★★ Paradise Valley/Larch Valley. A rewarding and challenging full-day hike, you'll hike below mounts Temple and Lefroy, and past Lake Annette, Horseshoe Meadows, and the "Giant's Staircase" waterfall, then over Sentinel Pass and down

The rushing Paradise Creek in Paradise Valley.

through Larch Valley to Moraine Lake—all superb highlights. The trail ends at a different parking lot from where it begins, so you'll need to organize a shuttle. Parks Canada often requires hikers to stay in groups of six or more due to bear activity in the area. *17km (11 miles) each way. Strenuous. Elevation gain is 880m (2,887 ft.). 6–7 hr. Trail head is 2.5km (1.5 miles) south on the Moraine Lake Rd. from Lake Louise Rd., in the Paradise Valley lot, on the right side of the road. Map p 140.*

★★★ **Plain of the Six Glaciers.** If you have time for only one half-day hike in Lake Louise, take this route through postcard-worthy scenery as it makes its way around Lake Louise and below mounts Victoria and Lefroy. It empties into

Hiking through the Plain of the Six Glaciers.

a harsh glacier- and avalanche-scoured terrain before climbing into a lush meadow, where you can stop at the historic Plain of the Six Glaciers Teahouse for a warm drink and snack. From the summit of a small moraine, you'll have the glaciers spread out before you. *5.3km (3.3 miles) each way. Moderate. Elevation gain 365m (1,198 ft.). 4–5 hr. round-trip. Trail head is Lake Louise Shoreline trail in front of Fairmont Chateau Lake Louise hotel. Map p 140.*

Saddleback Pass. The trail takes you to a stupendous view of the colossal Mt. Temple from a pass between Saddle and Fairview mountains. Heading out along the lower slopes of Mt. Fairview, the trail switchbacks up to a flower-filled meadow. It's steep, so bring poles to ease the trip down. Continue a bit farther to Fairview's summit for a mile-high view of Lake Louise. *3.7km (2.3 miles) one-way to pass. Moderate to strenuous. Elevation gain is 595m (1,952 ft.). 4 hr. round-trip. Trail head is on the south shore of Lake Louise to the right of the old guide's cabin. Map p 140.*

Icefields Parkway Hikes
kids Bow Glacier Falls. When the Bow Glacier retreated, it left behind a majestic 120m (394-ft.) waterfall that simply hints at the massive icefield above it. The trail is broad and scenic alongside the

flats skirting Bow Lake, a Rocky Mountain gem. At the western shore of the lake, there are views of the stunning Crowfoot and Bow glaciers. Only 100 years ago, the Bow Glacier extended to cover the entire Bow Valley. *4.7km (2.9 miles) each way. Easy. Elevation gain 95m (312 ft.). 3 hr. round-trip. Trail head is beside Num-Ti-Jah Lodge 36km (22 miles) north of the Lake Louise junction on Icefields Pkwy. 93. Map p 140.*

★ **Helen Lake.** With tall peaks, alpine meadows, lakes, and wide views, this trail is diverse enough to draw you enthusiastically around every corner. This is a relatively quick and pain-free way to access the high alpine environment. The lakeside meadows draw friendly hoary marmots. Check out the view of the Crowfoot Glacier. *6km (3.7 miles) each way. Moderate. Elevation gain 455m (1,493 ft.). 4 hr. round-trip. Trail head is across the highway from the Crowfoot Glacier Viewpoint, 33km (21 miles) north of the Lake Louise junction on Icefields Pkwy. 93. Map p 140.*

★ **Nigel Pass.** On this rewarding hike that tops out on a rocky 2,195m (7,201-ft.) ridge marking the

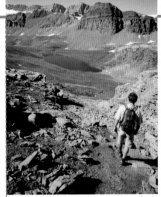

A hiker crosses a creek at Helen Lake.

boundary between Banff and Jasper national parks, you'll have great views of the Columbia Icefield. East of the pass, you can scramble over rocks to catch sight of the Brazeau River and the waterfall along the rocky north wall of Nigel Pass. *7.2km (4.5 miles) each way. Moderate. Elevation gain 365m (1,198 ft.). 5 hr. round-trip. Trail head is 2.5km (1.5 miles) north of the "Big Bend" switchback (114km/71 miles north of the Lake Louise junction) or 8.5km (5¼ miles) south of the Banff–Jasper boundary on the Icefields Pkwy. 93.*

Traveling Safely in Bear Country

Banff National Park is home to both black and grizzly bears. You could see a bear from your car, from your hotel, or even while out exploring the mountains on foot. Be prepared! Avoid having an encounter with a bear while hiking by making your presence well known so as not to surprise the bear—sing, talk, clap your hands, call "Hey Bear!" every few minutes while you hike, especially in densely forested areas or when crossing avalanche paths. Carry bear spray and know how to use it. And keep your eyes and ears open at all times.

  If you see a bear, try not to panic. Speak loudly and firmly to the bear and try to appear large by waving your arms. Back away slowly: do not run! For more information, visit www.pc.gc.ca/banff-bears.

Parker Ridge is a direct route to stunning views.

Parking lot is on northeast side of the highway. Map p 140.

★★★ **Parker Ridge.** The best short day hike in the Icefields Parkway area, this high and open trail takes you high up and straight into the heart of the unforgiving alpine zone. In summer—which can last only a few weeks up here—the meadows turn a brilliant red with heather. Once you reach the summit, enjoy views of the Saskatchewan Glacier (the glacier that reaches the farthest out into a valley in the Columbia Icefield) below you. *2.7km (1.7 miles) each way. Moderate. Elevation gain 250m (820 ft.). 3 hr. round-trip. Trail head is in parking lot on the west side of the*

Icefields Pkwy. 93, 4km (2.5 miles) south of the Banff–Jasper park boundary. Map p 140.

Peyto Lake/Bow Summit. This is the most popular short hike along the Icefields Parkway. Escape the crowds by continuing on to the Bow Summit lookout; then hike down to the lake for an almost bird's-eye view of the Bow River's source. This trail takes you through what is known as the transition zone; what begins as a thick forest soon becomes a stunted one, getting sparser and sparser until you come to an area where there isn't a single tree growing. *3.1km (1.9 miles) each way. Easy. Elevation gain 230m (755 ft.). 2 hr. round-trip. Trail head is Bow Summit parking lot 41km (25 miles) north of the Lake Louise junction on Icefields Pkwy. 93. Map p 140.*

★★★ **Wilcox Pass.** Starting just across the border in Jasper National Park, this trail gives you an almost bird's-eye view of the spectacular Columbia Icefield from the edge of a gorgeous alpine valley. It's an incredibly rewarding—albeit popular—trail since it's mostly above the treeline, offering nearly nonstop views and plenty of wildflowers in August. *12km (7.4 miles) return. Moderate. Elevation gain*

A hiker pauses at Wilcox Pass, looking at the Columbia Icefield.

Backpacking: The Ultimate Rocky Mountain Experience

It's a challenging undertaking—most people just starting to backpack will find the routes in Banff National Park demanding, because of the mountainous terrain. And you must be very well organized with what you bring on the trip. But a night under the stars in the Banff backcountry promises the ultimate Rocky Mountain high. The peak hiking season is from early July to mid-September, and be sure to reserve your campsites ahead of time. There are dozens of possible trips, but the three listed below are my favorites!

335m (1,099 ft.). 5 hr. round-trip. Trail head is 2.5km (1.6 miles) south of the Icefields Centre on Icefields Pkwy. 93 at the Wilcox Pass campground. Map p 140.

Backpacking Hikes
★★ Egypt Lake/Shadow Lake. This is the most popular backpacking area in Banff National Park, a multi-day exploration of Banff's highest-elevation hiking routes. With a series of passes along the Continental Divide, encompassing cliffs, meadows, and lake-dotted alpine cirques, this trail takes you through some quintessential Canadian Rockies landscape. *40km (25 miles) return. Moderate. Elevation gain 790m (2,592 ft.). 2–3 days. Trail head is Sunshine Village ski area.*

kids Glacier Lake. This overnight trip isn't too strenuous and gets you into the Icefields Parkway backcountry. It's a nice outing for families, since the hike is quite flat and the elevation is relatively low. The beginning elevation is 1,450m (4,757 ft.) and you gain 210m (689 ft.) over the course of the trip. *8.9km (5.5 miles) each way. Easy. Elevation gain 210m (689 ft.). 2 days. Trail head is on west side of Icefields Pkwy. 93, 1.2km (.8 mile) north of the*

junction with Hwy. 11, near Saskatchewan Crossing.

★★★ Sunshine Meadows/ Mt. Assiniboine. Showcasing the spectacularly colorful Sunshine Meadows and Mt. Assiniboine region, this route covers high alpine terrain, crosses dramatic passes, and runs alongside picturesque lakes. Head over Citadel Pass to admire Mt. Assiniboine (the highest mountain in Banff National Park, also known as the "Matterhorn of the Rockies"), in British Columbia's Mt. Assiniboine Provincial Park. *62km (39 miles) return. Moderate to strenuous. Elevation gain 655m (2,149 ft.). 3–6 days. Trail head is Sunshine Village ski area. Map p 140.*

Mt. Assiniboine is known as the "Matterhorn of the Rockies."

Summer Sports

Canoeing
Moraine Lake 9
Lake Louise 5
Bow River at Banff 14

Climbing
"Back of the Lake"
  at Lake Louise 3
Mount Athabasca 1
Mount Assiniboine 27
Via Ferrata 8

Fishing
Vermillion Lakes 11
Upper Bow River 6

Golf
Fairmont Banff
  Springs Golf course 20

Helicopter Tours
Alpine Helicopters 25
Rockies Heli Tours 2

Horseback Riding
Spray River 23
Martin Stables 16

Rafting
Kicking Horse River 10
Kananaskis River 26
Bow River 18

Swimming
Upper Hot Spring 21
Johnson Lake 24
Sally Borden Centre 17

Biking
Vermillion Lakes 12
Banff Springs Golf
  Course drive 19
Spray River Loop 22
Bow River Loop 4

Birdwatching
Cave and Basin
  March 15
Fenland Trail 13
Bow River Bridge
  and Castle Junction 7

(i) Information
■ Point of Interest

There are many activities to choose from during summertime in Banff. This isn't a place for loungers. Besides hiking, give yourself a chance to sample a few of the adventures listed below. Get out and try something new!

A mountain biker rides along the Spray River Loop.

Biking

With more than 190km (118 miles) of mountain-bike trails and numerous options for road biking, Banff is a friendly place for two wheels. Bike season runs from May to October. Note that not all hiking trails are open to bikers.

You can rent both road and mountain bikes in Banff National Park at **Soul Ski and Bike** (203 Bear St.; ☎ 403/760-1650) and **Banff Adventures** (211 Bear St.; ☎ 403/762-4554), which also has kids' bikes, trailers, and strollers. In Lake Louise, rent bikes at **Wilson Mountain Sports** (p 21).

Good routes around the Banff Townsite area include the Banff Springs Golf Course drive and the Vermillion Lakes via the paved Fenland Trail. When you head out from the townsite, take the Bow Valley Parkway (Hwy. 93A). There's much

Share the Trail

Bike trails in Banff National Park are also hiking and horseback-riding trails. Expect to encounter people using the trail in other ways. Ride in control and always be prepared to stop. Slow down when you come upon a hiker. A friendly greeting will make them aware of your presence. Bikes can spook horses: When passing a horse, let the rider know you are coming. If a horse approaches you, move to the side of the trail, stop your bike, and let the horse pass. If you have a chance to stop and chat a little, ask the rider about the trail conditions ahead.

less traffic than on the Trans-Canada Highway (Hwy. 1). If you're up at Lake Louise, try the old Great Divide Road, which leads into Yoho National Park—a quiet ride through mountain scenery.

Mountain biking is permitted on only a select number of the trails in Banff National Park. You are subject to fines if you are caught biking on hiking-only trails. In the Banff Town-site area, the best ride for begin-ners and families is the 13km (7.8-mile) Spray River Loop. Near Lake Louise, families with kids will enjoy the relatively flat but very sce-nic 7.1km (4.4-mile) Bow River Loop, which leaves from the Lake Louise Campground. There are interpretive signs along the trail.

More advanced bikers will find thrills on the steep and narrow Stoney Squaw Loop or along the winding Toe Trail, near the Hoodoos.

Bird-Watching
Birding is a great activity for visitors of all ages. More than 260 species pass through the Canadian Rockies annually. Pick up a brochure from the Banff Information Centre in Banff Townsite (224 Banff Ave.; ☎ 403/762-1550). Great spots close to the Town of Banff include Cave and Basin March and Fenland Trail. Look for an osprey nest on the Bow River Bridge and Castle Junction.

Canoeing
To canoe is to be Canadian, it is said. There are boathouses where you can rent canoes at both Moraine Lake and Lake Louise. The Moraine Lake Lodge's boathouse (14km/8¾ miles south of Lake Lou-ise on Moraine Lake Rd.; ☎ 403/522-3733) rents canoes for $40 per hour. The Fairmont Chateau Lake Louise (111 Lake Louise Dr.; ☎ 403/522-3511) rents canoes for $65 per hour. In the Town of Banff, rent a canoe at the **Banff Canoe Club**

Climbers take on the "Back of the Lake" route at Lake Louise.

(end of Wolf St.; www.banffcanoe club.com; ☎ 403/762-5005) for $36 per hour, where you can paddle straight into the placid Vermillion Lakes.

Be prepared if you're planning on canoeing the Bow River; experi-ence is recommended, particularly in the section between Castle Junc-tion and Banff, where there's a Class III rapid. The paddle from Banff to Canmore is intermediate-level and requires route-finding skills.

Climbing & Mountaineering
Visitors to Banff who've taken the time and energy to learn the ropes enjoy this highly technical sport. There are no specific regulations governing climbing or mountaineer-ing in Banff National Park; however, Parks Canada does suggest you contact the Banff Warden's office (in Banff ☎ 403/762-1470; in Lake Louise ☎ 403/522-1220) for more information before you head out.

There are a number of excellent rock-climbing locations in Banff, including the "Back of the Lake," at Lake Louise. Classic mountain climbs include mounts Athabasca and Assiniboine—both are for experienced climbers only.

For advice on planning a climbing trip, contact the **Alpine Club of Canada** (☎ 403/678-3200; www.alpineclubofcanada.ca) or the **Association of Canadian Mountain Guides** (☎ 403/678-2885; www.acmg.ca). For private lessons and guiding, contact Canada's premier mountaineering school, **Yamnuska Inc.** (☎ 403/678-4164; www.yamnuska.com).

Via Ferrata

High on the ridges above Mt. Norquay is a unique opportunity to scale big mountains and get up really high. A Via Ferrata is a series of ladders, cables, and a suspension bridge that takes you (along with a certified guide) up to the beautiful Cliffhouse Bistro. The climb isn't as hard as it sounds, and it's great fun. No experience needed. *At Mt. Norquay. 2 Mt. Norquay Rd., Banff. ☎ 844/667-7829. www.banffnorquay.com. From $139/person. Departures throughout the day from 9am–3pm.*

Fishing

You need a permit to fish in Banff National Park. Pick one up at the Banff Information Centre in Banff Townsite (224 Banff Ave.; ☎ 403/762-1550). National Park fishing

A thrilling day for a climber on the Via Ferrata.

permits cost $10 daily. An annual permit costs $34. While there are lots of lakes here, few have any fish left in them. However, the Bow River is one of the world's finest fly-fishing rivers and is the only area in Banff National Park open year-round.

Banff Fishing Unlimited (☎ 403/762-4936; www.banff-fishing.com) specializes in year-round fly-fishing, spin casting, and trophy lake-trout fishing. Their guides know all the secrets. **Alpine Anglers** (☎ 403/762-8223; www.alpineanglers.com) offers top-notch instruction in the mild sensibilities of fly-fishing on the pristine, turquoise waters of the Bow River.

The Fairmont Banff Springs Hotel and the Banff Springs Golf Course.

Riding horses near Banff.

Golfing

The Fairmont Banff Springs Hotel's 27-hole **Stanley Thompson Course** is world famous (405 Spray Ave.; ☎ 403/762-6801). The course has three tee-offs and an amazingly scenic location along the Spray and Bow rivers, beneath Mt. Rundle. It's expensive but legendary, and open to the public (you don't have to be a guest at the hotel to play a round). Course fees range from $191 in May and October and $239 from June through September, including cart. There's also a 9-hole course. Watch for geese and elk!

Helicopter Tours

To get the ultimate bird's-eye view of the jaw-droppingly beautiful Rockies, you have to step just outside the boundary of Banff National Park. Near the Icefields Centre, **Rockies Heli Tours** (☎ 888/844-3514 or 403/721-2100; www.rockies heli.com) has flights starting at $189 per person. **Alpine Helicopters** (☎ 403/678-4802; www.alpine helicopters.com) takes off just east of Banff in Canmore and flies to Mt. Assiniboine and back in 30 unforgettable minutes ($299 per person). They also have heli-hiking day tours starting at $489.

Horseback Riding

Riding a horse in the Canadian Rockies is as logical as riding a camel in the Sahara Desert. Saddling up not only lets you explore the cowboy heritage of the Rockies, it also lets you wind your way into parts of the Banff backcountry you might not otherwise have seen. Having said this, only a select few trails in Banff National Park are able to accommodate horses, so I recommend taking a trip organized by a local outfitter. They'll show you a

Saddle Up & Head High

If you're not sure about long days of hiking and carrying your own packs but you still want to explore the backcountry of Banff, consider an overnight horseback trip. From early May to late October, trail rides range from 1 night to 1 week. Some outfitters combine guided trail rides with stays at rustic but comfortable backcountry lodges, while others include overnights in wilderness tents situated in truly spectacular settings. This is one of the best ways to see the back corners of Banff—with considerably less effort than backpacking. For trips from 2 to 4 days, ranging from $639 to $956, try **Banff Trail Riders** (132 Banff Ave.; ☎ 403/762-4551 or 800/661-8352; www.horseback.com). Starting at the Lake Louise Corral, **Timberline Tours** (☎ 403/522-3743; www.timberlinetours. ca) has overnight trips starting at $470 per person.

Rafting down the Bow River.

good ol' time, while keeping you on course.

Timberline Tours (☎ 403/522-3743; www.timberlinetours.ca) leads scenic trips at Lake Louise. A half-day outing is between $129 and $169, while overnight trips start at $510. **Banff Trail Riders** (132 Banff Ave., ☎ 800/661-8352 or 403/762-4551; www.horseback.com) has a corral at the Fairmont Banff Springs Hotel, where they run 1-hour tours along the Spray River ($54). They have another corral at Martin Stables (located on the banks of the Bow River across from Banff Townsite), where 5- to 7-hour trips head

Going for a swim at Johnson Lake.

into the Sundance Range ($249). They also organize wonderfully fun wilderness cookouts, which include a Cowboy Cookout Lunch ($119) and an Evening Trailride, where they serve a large Western barbecue dinner ($129). All prices are per person.

Rafting
The gnarliest rapids in the Canadian Rockies are west of Banff on the Kicking Horse River (p 111) and east of Banff on the Kananaskis River. From the Town of Banff, you can hop on a gentle float trip down the Bow River. It's great for families. **Rocky Mountain Raft Tours** (☎ 403/762-3632; www.banffraft tours.com) departs from just below Bow Falls and drops you at Canmore for $85 for adults, $40 for youth 15 and under.

Swimming
The spring-fed outdoor pools at the historic Banff Upper Hot Springs (p 5) make for a memorable dip any time of year. On a hot summer day, join the locals for an afternoon swim at Johnson Lake on the Minnewanka Loop. Throughout the year, the nicest indoor pool in Banff is at the sunny Banff Centre's **Sally Borden Centre** (St. Julien Rd., ☎ 403/762-6450).

Winter Sports

Legend

- ▲ Campground
- ⛽ Gasoline
- ✚ Hospital/First Aid
- ⓘ Information
- ◻ Point of Interest
- 🎿 Ski Area

Alpine Skiing
Lake Louise Resort **1**
Mt. Norquay **12**
Sunshine Village **13**

Cross-Country Skiing
Golf Course Trail/
 Spray River Loop **9**
Pipestone **2**

Dog Sledding
Divide Road **3**
Spray Lakes **15**

Ice Climbing
Yamnuska Inc. **14**

Ice Walks
Johnston Canyon **11**

Ice Skating
Fairmont Banff
 Springs Hotel **8**
Lake Louise **4**
Vermillion Lakes **7**

Snowshoeing
Fairview Lookout **5**
Fenland Trail **6**
Moose Meadows **10**

Winter is breathtaking in the Canadian Rockies, in both beauty and temperature. Days can drop to –15 °C (5 °F) or lower, but you'll be too busy sampling the many adventures available—some you may have never experienced before—to care. Dress warmly, keep a pair of gloves and hat nearby, and make the most of the legendarily clear and sunny days and the starry nights.

Alpine Skiing

Lake Louise Ski Resort. The views here will have you picking your jaw up off the glistening powder snow. Easy to access and full of varied terrain, Louise keeps folks loyal. Beginners will find a friendly ski and snowboard school, as well as some lovely green runs to get started. Head straight to the top of the Grizzly Express Gondola for more advanced blue runs. Larch is a great place for intermediates. Expert skiers should take to the Top of the World "Six-Pack" Chair and then the Summit Platter, and enjoy powder bowls like West Bowl and Boomerang. There is a terrain park with jumps, obstacles, and railings. Cozy and rustic Temple Lodge, tucked in behind the resort below Whitehorn Mountain, is a good lunch restaurant while Whitehorn Lodge has amazing views. *Follow Whitehorn Rd. off the Trans-Canada Hwy. 1 at the Lake Louise exit.* ☎ *800/258-7669 or 403/522-3555. www.skilouise.com.*

Mt. Norquay. At Banff's doorstep, this small resort has produced many world-class ski racers. It's got plenty of steep runs, and it's intimate and convenient, particularly their economical ski-by-the-hour deals (starting with 2 hr.), meaning you don't have to spend the entire day here to feel like you've gotten your money's worth. This is particularly appealing for beginners and families. On a powder day, head straight to the Memorial Bowl. It's open for night skiing on Fridays 5pm to 10pm. *At the end of Mt. Norquay Dr.* ☎ *403/762-4421. www.banffnorquay.com.*

Sunshine Village. Tucked high in the alpine zone in a series of scenic bowls centered around a "village" with a hotel, day lodge, ski school, and gondola station, Sunshine gets fabulous snow and has an

Skiing the steep runs at Mt. Norquay.

Sunshine Village ski resort is known for its excellent snow and abundant space.

abundance of space. It stays open weeks later than the other resorts in Banff, usually until the third week of May. Strawberry and Standish chairs are great for beginners. The Continental Divide has amazing views for intermediate skiers. Goat's Eye Mountain is great for advanced skiers. And only experts need attempt the aptly named Delirium Dive. Advanced snowboarders will find a lot of flat terrain at Sunshine, but the terrain park has grown steadily over the years and is a fun spot for catching some air. *8km (5 miles) west of Banff Townsite at the end of Sunshine Rd.* ☎ *800/661-1676 or 403/762-6500. www.skibanff.com.*

Cross-Country (Nordic) Skiing

A wonderful way to explore the park in winter, cross-country skiing promises great exercise, views, and solitude, if you're seeking it. There are more than 80km (50 miles) of managed trails in Banff National Park, many of them within a half-hour drive of Banff Townsite. The cross-country ski season runs from December to March.

Parks Canada regularly updates trail reports online at www.pc.gc.ca/banff and ☎ 403/762-1550 for Banff Townsite area or ☎ 403/522-3833 for Lake Louise.

Rent cross-country equipment at the **Ski Stop** (see below). In Lake

Ski Big Three

Ski packages that allow you to spend a day at each of Banff's three resorts are offered by the Ski Banff/Lake Louise partnership (P.O. Box 1085, Banff, AB T1L 1H9; ☎ 877/754-7080 or 403/762-4561; www.skibig3.com). Packages include hotel and lift tickets at each of the three resorts. The lift ticket prices for adults range from $258 for 3 out of 4 days to $475 for 6 out of 8 days. It's a great deal and an excellent way to sample Banff's outstanding skiing. You can also book a guide or instructor to accompany you each day.

Rent downhill skis and equipment, as well as snowboarding equipment, in Banff at **the Ski Stop** (203A Bear St.; ☎ 403/762-1650) or at the Fairmont Banff Springs Hotel (405 Spray Ave.; ☎ 403/762-5333). In Lake Louise, rent skis, snowshoes, and snowboards at **Wilson Mountain Sports** (p 21). For a ski or snowboard tune-up, try **Ultimate Ski and Ride** (206 Banff Ave.; ☎ 403/762-0547) or **Monod Sports** (p 87).

Steep & Deep Runs Near Banff

Within a few hours of the Town of Banff, there are two other amazing ski resorts worth a visit, both in the Columbia Valley in British Columbia next door. **Panorama Mountain Resort** (from Hwy. 95, turn west at the Town of Invermere and right onto Panorama Dr., 18km/11 miles to uphill; ☎ 800/663-2929 or 250/342-6941; www.panoramaresort.com) has a whopping 1,220 vertical meters (4,000 vertical ft.) and some deliciously long cruiser runs great for high-level intermediates. There's a cozy village of condos and hotels at the base. At **Kicking Horse Mountain Resort** (from Hwy. 95, turn west at blue sign in downtown Golden, 13km/8 miles uphill; ☎ 866/754-5425 or 250/439-5400; www.kickinghorseresort.com), the snow is famously so light it's called "champagne powder." The resort will appeal mainly to advanced skiers who aren't intimidated by steep terrain and deep snow. Most of the development here has happened since 2002, and the vibe is diehard and earthy.

Louise; rent skis and snowshoes at **Wilson Mountain Sports** (p 21).

The Golf Course Trail has ungroomed trails that are wide open and easy for beginners. There are no defined trails and little elevation gain here, but it's a good place to get a feel for the sport. At Moraine Lake Road, there are 8km (5 miles) of double trackset trails, ideal for a good workout. Flat and wide, trails branch off to the west on the slopes of Mt. Fairview.

The Spray River Loop is a 12km (7.8 mile) trail leading behind the Fairmont Banff Springs Hotel with a 200m (656-ft.) elevation gain. Tracks are set for both skate-skiing and classic skiing. It's a good place if you want to go fast. The Pipestone Loops are a wide range of trails across the highway from the Lake Louise village, from 1.9 to 12km (1.2–7.8 miles). All are trackset. Check at the Lake Louise Visitors Centre for updates on trail conditions.

Dog Sledding
Just over the border from Banff National Park, another classic winter tradition matches tourists up with friendly huskies for a mush across a frozen lake. It's exhilarating. Try **Snowy Owl Sled Dog Tours** (104–602 Bow Valley Pkwy., Canmore; ☎ 403/678-4369; www.snowyowltours.com). For mushing tours near Lake Louise, contact **Kingmik Dog Sled Tours** (☎ 403/763-8887; www.kingmikdogsledtours.com).

Ice Climbing
The frozen waterfalls of Banff National Park offer some of the finest

Snowshoeing near Lake Louise.

The Great Outdoors

Banff offers some of the finest ice climbing in the world.

ice climbing in the world. It's an extreme sport that requires proper preparation, but it's also an exhilarating experience—technical, exciting, and beautiful. Learn to climb with the guides at **Yamnuska** (☎ 403/678-4164; www.yamnuska.com).

Ice Skating

There are a number of places where you can skate outdoors under the winter sky. It's an exhilarating activity that's popular with families. Try the Vermillion Lakes or Johnson Lake, both just outside the Town of Banff, in the early winter before the

snow starts to pile up. There's also a public outdoor rink behind the Fairmont Banff Springs Hotel. At the Fairmont Chateau Lake Louise, there is an outdoor rink on the lake with a spectacular ice castle built right on top. It's a very scenic and romantic place to skate.

Ice Walks

The frozen walls at Johnston Canyon become a winter wonderland, thanks to ice cleats and the guides from **Banff Adventures** (211 Bear St.; ☎ 403/762-4554; www.banffadventures.com), who take visitors out for a 4-hour intimate discovery of ice.

Snowshoeing

Strapping on a pair of snowshoes opens up miles and miles of possibilities in Banff, from short strolls near town to big backcountry bowls. Most snowshoe trails follow summer hiking trails—be sure to avoid cross-country trails (groomed or not groomed), as it interferes with the skiing, and be avalanche-aware. Near the townsite, try the flat Fenland Trail. Two other great spots are Moose Meadows on the Bow Valley Parkway and Fairview Lookout above Lake Louise. Well-priced guided snowshoeing trips are also organized by **Lake Louise Ski Resort** (☎ 877/956-8473 or 403/522-3555; www.skilouise.com). ●

Ice skating outside the Fairmont Chateau Lake Louise.

Before You Go

Tourist Office

The **Canadian Tourism Commission** (☎ 604/638-8300; www.canada. travel) and **Travel Alberta,** 999 8th St., Calgary (☎ 800/252-3782 or 780/427-4321; www.travelalberta. com) are useful sources of information. The Travel Alberta site is inspiring and helps you understand the breadth of attractions in this province. You can also check out the website for the **Banff Lake Louise Tourism Bureau,** Ste. 375, Cascade Plaza, Banff Avenue (☎ 403/762-8421; www.banfflakelouise.com).

The Best Time to Go

Unless you are a skier, summer is the most enjoyable time of the year to be in the Canadian Rockies. However, it's also the most crowded and expensive time. Most hotels double their prices during the high season, which stretches from June through September. So consider the "shoulder seasons." In **June,** the days are luxuriously long and you can catch the early wildflowers in bloom and perhaps even some migrating caribou. In **September,** aspen and larch trees turn golden, but the midday temperature stays gloriously warm.

    The Canadian Rockies are also a great destination in winter, by turns cozy, romantic, and peaceful, but also brimming with fun outdoor activities. Banff's star ski resorts—**Sunshine Village, Mount Norquay,** and **Lake Louise**—are among the best in North America. Everything in the Town of Banff stays open year-round, with many hotels dropping their prices substantially during the winter season, which runs from **December to late March.** There are often road closures

throughout the Canadian Rockies due to snowfall, especially in the high mountain passes.

Festivals & Special Events

JAN Ice Magic Festival (☎ 403/762-8421; www.banfflakelouise.com) is a stellar ice-carving competition held on the frozen shores of Lake Louise.

MARCH Lake Louise Loppet (☎ 403/289-0386; www.calgaryski club.org) is a family-friendly annual cross-country ski race that also attracts Olympians and National Ski Team members.

APRIL The longest-running ski race in the Canadian Rockies happens each year at Mount Norquay—the **Bruno Engler Memorial Race.** It brings out old-timers and young hot-shots, and lots of locals dressed in retro ski costumes. (☎ 403/762-7703; www.banffnorquay.com).

MAY Say farewell to winter with a splash at Sunshine Village's **Slush Cup Beach Party Weekend** (www. skibanff.com), the last weekend of the ski season. Outdoor concerts, a beer garden, and wild folks ski jumping across puddles are highlights.

MAY–AUG From drama and opera to jazz and classical music, the **Banff Summer Arts Festival** (☎ 403/762-6301; www.banffcentre.ca) showcases the best in a variety of artistic areas. If you are an arts lover, don't miss this.

JUNE Teams of 15 runners journey across the Icefields Parkway from Banff to Jasper as part of the annual **Banff to Jasper Relay** (www.bjr.ca).

JULY Held on July 1, **Canada Day** is the anniversary of the signing of the "British North America Act" with the United Kingdom, which created

Previous Page: A welcome sign on the outskirts of Banff.

AVERAGE MONTHLY TEMPERATURES & RAINFALL

	JAN	FEB	MAR	APR	MAY	JUNE
High °F/°C	23/–5	32/0	40/4	49/9	57/14	72/20
Low °F/°C	5/–15	13/–11	18/–8	27/–3	31/2	41/5
Days of precipitation	12	10	11	11	16	18

	JULY	AUG	SEPT	OCT	NOV	DEC
High °F/°C	82/25	80/24	66/17	50/10	32/1	23/–5
Low °F/°C	45/7	44/7	38/3	31/–1	18/–8	7/–14
Days of precipitation	19	14	11	11	13	12

the united country of Canada. Following a free pancake breakfast in Banff's Central Park, pick a good spot on Banff Avenue to take in the late afternoon parade, with cowboys and marching bands. In the evening, there's live music in the park and fireworks light up the sky.

AUG Over the first weekend in August, the peaks form an amazing backdrop for 3 days of music at the annual **Canmore Folk Music Festival** (☎ 403/678-2524; www.canmorefolkfestival.com), Alberta's longest-running folk music festival.

AUG Since 1926, Jasper has hosted the **Jasper Heritage Pro Rodeo** (☎ 780/852-4622; www.jasperheritagerodeo.com), featuring bareback, saddle bronc, steer wrestling, and barrel racing. There's a Western dance, barbecue, and kid's rodeo held in town.

AUG Banff's many heritage buildings welcome visitors during **Doors Open Banff** (☎ 403/762-8421; www.doorsopenalberta.ca) for self-guided heritage tours.

SEPT A Banff tradition that draws runners from across Western Canada, **Melissa's Road Race** (www.melissasroadrace.ca) has a 10K (6.2 mile) and 22K (13.7 mile) road route, with proceeds going to the Banff community. It sells out months ahead of time, but spectators can catch the action at the finish line at the Banff Recreational Grounds.

OCT–NOV Each year, the Banff Centre hosts the **Banff Mountain Film and Book Festival** (☎ 403/762-6301; www.banffcentre.ca) celebrating the spirit of those who live in the mountains. If you're a keen armchair adventurer, it's best to buy a weekend pass, which will get you into plenty of screenings as well as to hear guest speakers and rub shoulders with some of the finest adventurers from around the world.

NOV–DEC From a World Cup Alpine ski race to a Santa Claus Parade, winter gets a kick-start during the annual **WinterStart Festival** (☎ 403/762-8421; www.banfflakelouise.com).

The Weather

Despite the Canadian Rockies' northerly latitude, the climate actually resembles that of the Rocky Mountains south of the United States border because the altitude isn't as high as it is in the U.S. Rockies. Snow at lower elevations usually disappears by May, but sometimes hangs around the higher elevations well into the summer. Although it often rains for at least a week in June, and you can expect a cold rain or wet snowfall in July, the summer climate is generally very pleasant, with warm days and low humidity. Evenings almost always require a sweater. Rain clouds often gather along the Continental Divide, so don't be disappointed to come all the way here and not be able to see the high peaks right away. July temperatures typically hit 68° to 77°F (20°–25°C). Spring and fall days are usually fine and bright, though evenings can be cool.

In January, though the lows can drop way down to –22°F (–30°C), the winter sunshine and blue skies are the stuff of legend.

Useful Websites
In addition to the websites at the opening of this chapter, check out:

- **www.parkscanada.gc.ca:** Incredibly useful information on all of the area's national parks.

- **www.mountainnature.com:** Great information on the natural history of the area.

- **www.banff.com:** A site with event listings, virtual tours, weather updates, and listings for everything from restaurants to ski-rental shops.

- **www.banff.ca:** The site for the Town of Banff has useful details for visitors, including information on the public-transit system.

Cell Phones
The cellular phone coverage in the Canadian Rockies has improved dramatically. In the Town of Banff, as in other towns like Canmore,

Lake Louise, and Jasper, coverage is good. In between these spots, though, it is not consistent and service often drops. For example, your coverage will likely cut out as you drive from Banff to Lake Louise. Phones using CDMA network technology—currently the most common type in use in both Canada and the U.S.—will work in Canada in places with reception. GSM/GPRS phones—the dominant standard pretty much everywhere else—also work here, thanks to roaming agreements. Before leaving home, be sure to update your phone's roaming software to assure good connectivity. And check with your provider to see what kind of international usage fees may apply. For information on land lines and international calls, see "Telephones" in the *Fast Facts* section below.

Car Rentals
Most visitors to Banff and Jasper national parks will fly to either Calgary or Edmonton and rent a car to get to the parks. Though frequent and good shuttle service is available from the Calgary International Airport to several locations around Banff (see "By Plane" below), it's a good idea to rent a car to get around for the duration of your trip.

Getting **There**

By Plane
Both the **Calgary International Airport** (☎ 877/254-7427 or 403/735-1200; www.calgaryairport.com) and the **Edmonton International Airport** (☎ 800/268-7134; www.edmontonairports.com) service the Canadian Rockies. If you are

heading to Banff National Park, fly to Calgary and from there take the **Banff Airporter** (☎ 888/449-2901 or 403/762-3330; www.banffairporter.com; $60.50 one-way or $121 round-trip). Banff is 129km (80 miles) west of Calgary. It's about 90 minutes by car from the airport.

If you want to visit Jasper National Park first, fly to Edmonton (363km/225 miles east of Jasper; a 4-hr. trip by car). Many people visiting Jasper go first to Banff via Calgary and then drive north. Others do the trip in reverse.

By Car

If you're driving into Banff National Park from the east, take the **Trans-Canada Highway (Hwy. 1)** west from Calgary. The park's eastern gate is 129km (80 miles) west of the **Calgary International Airport,** just west of the town of Canmore. If you are coming to Banff from the west, you have two options. From central British Columbia, you can take the Trans-Canada Highway east via the town of **Golden, BC,** and Yoho National Park, and enter Banff just west of the village of Lake Louise.

The other option, from southeastern British Columbia, is to take Hwy. 93 north into Banff via the town of **Radium Hot Springs, BC,** and Kootenay National Park. See chapter 5 for more information on planning a side trip to Golden, BC, or Radium Hot Springs, BC.

If you're approaching the parks from the city of Edmonton, which is to the north, you'll get to Jasper National Park first. Take **Hwy. 16** (the Yellowhead Hwy.) west to Jasper National Park's eastern gate (363km/225 miles west of Edmonton International Airport). From north-central British Columbia, you can take Hwy. 16 east to Jasper National Park via **Prince George, BC,** and Mount Robson Provincial Park.

Vancouver is 858km (532 miles) west of Banff and 863km (535 miles) west of Jasper.

By Train

VIA Rail Canada (☎ 888/842-7245; www.viarail.ca) services Jasper National Park on its Edmonton–Vancouver run, which takes about 16 hours direct. Most trains from major Canadian and U.S. centers connect to this route. Check with VIA Rail Canada or with **Amtrak** (☎ 800/872-7245; www.amtrak.com).

There is no VIA Rail Canada service to Banff or Calgary; however, **Rocky Mountaineer Railtours** (☎ 877/460-3200; www.rockymountaineer.com) has a stunning overnight trip that departs from Vancouver and stops in either Banff or Jasper. (You select your destination at the changeover in Kamloops, BC.)

By Bus
Greyhound Bus Lines (☎ 800/661-8747; www.greyhound.ca) has multiple arrivals daily through Banff and Jasper going both east and west. Their routes from Vancouver to Calgary stop in Canmore, Banff, Field and Golden.

Getting **Around**

By Bus
Banff's **ROAM** public bus system (☎ 403/762-0606; www.roamtransit.com) is very good and runs regularly throughout the day and will take you to the Sulphur Mountain gondola, the hot springs, the Fairmont Banff Springs Hotel and up Tunnel Mountain Road. There is also an hourly public bus to the nearby town of Canmore. Many Banff hotels offer free bus passes to

their guests to help fight congested roads in peak season. One-way fares start at $2.

By Shuttle

There are a number of shuttle services to help ease your travel between Banff and Jasper national parks. **Sundog Tours** (☎ 888/786-3641 or 780/852-4056; www.sundog tours.com) runs between Banff, Lake Louise, and Jasper daily (except from poor winter-driving days and from Nov–late Dec). Some daily departures hit all the major attractions along the way; others go directly from Jasper to Lake Louise or Banff. The Jasper–Banff trip costs $69 per adult and $39 per child 12 and under; the Jasper–Lake Louise trip costs $59 per adult and $35 per child.

By Car

If you are staying in the Town of Banff and not really planning on trips outside of it, you can take a shuttle from the Calgary airport and then walk, take the local ROAM public bus system, or a short cab ride to most attractions in town. However, if you plan on seeing any of the rest of the park, including Lake Louise, as well as making a trip to Jasper, then having your own vehicle is a major advantage. It can be hard to get to trail heads, although ski resorts run shuttles during the winter.

There is little to no public transport between main destinations in the Canadian Rockies, and taxi services are very expensive—not to mention restricting, since your movements are governed by their schedule. The roads are in good condition most of the year (you don't really need to rent an expensive four-wheel-drive sport-utility vehicle except during major snowstorms), and driving here is a relaxing way to soak up the gorgeous scenery.

The one downside of renting a car is that parking can be a problem in the Town of Banff and at Lake Louise. Stick to the big parking lots (in Banff there is a covered multi-story parkade on Bear St. between Caribou and Buffalo sts., in Lake Louise at the Samson Mall, and in Jasper beside the Heritage Railway Station). For more information, see chapter 4.

By RV

They're not for everyone, but most people who try it discover what a joy it is to travel by recreational vehicle. It affords a level of independence and comfort that car travel can't. And finding a quiet campground by a river is as close to the camping experience as you can get without giving up your pillow and mattress.

More than half of the campgrounds in Banff and Jasper national parks accommodate RVs, trailers, and camper vans, and you must stay in these designated areas. In addition to navigating around campgrounds, RVs (and their drivers) need to know how to get around town, too. In the Town of Banff, there is a trailer drop-off site in the industrial area at the northeast end of Banff Avenue. You can leave your trailer here and take the car or RV itself through the streets of town. There are also a number of larger parking lots that accommodate RVs, including one near the Mineral Springs Hospital on Gopher Street and another one across from the post office on Buffalo Street, along the Bow River.

Many people come to the Rockies in an RV they've rented at the airport in Edmonton or Calgary.

For RV rentals, contact **CanaDream** (2510 27th St. NE, Calgary, AB T1Y 7G1; ☎ 800/461-7368 or 403/291-1000; www.cana dream.com).

Fast **Facts**

ATMS Banff does have its share of Automated Teller Machines, which operate on the worldwide **Cirrus** (☎ 800/424-7787; www.mastercard.com), **PLUS** (☎ 800/843-7587; www.visa.com), and **Interac** (☎ 416/362-8550; www.interac.ca) networks. Be sure you know your personal identification number (PIN) before you leave home, and be sure your daily withdrawal limit will cover the amount of cash you'll need. Note that ATM fees can be higher for international transactions than for domestic. **Alberta Treasury's** branch is at 317 Banff Ave. (☎ 403/762-8505). In Lake Louise there is an ATM in Samson Mall (☎ 403/522-3678). The **Bank of Montreal** is at 107 Banff Ave. (☎ 403/762-2275), and the **Canadian Imperial Bank of Canada** (CIBC) is at 98 Banff Ave. (☎ 403/762-3317).

BANKING HOURS Banks are generally open Monday through Friday 9:30am to 4:30pm, though some branches have hours on weekends as well.

BIKE RENTALS Bike shops will likely try to rent you their most expensive bikes. If you're a beginner mountain biker, however, and will only be heading out on a few trails around town, you do not need a full-suspension bike. If you want to just cruise the main, paved, trails of the townsite, go for an inexpensive bike.

You can rent both road and mountain bikes in Banff National Park at **Soul Ski & Bike** (203 Bear St.; ☎ 403/760-1650; www.soulskiandbike.com). In addition to renting regular-size bikes for adult riders, **Banff Adventures** (211 Bear St.; ☎ 403/762-4554; www.banffadventures.com) rents kids' bikes, trailers, and strollers, too. In Lake Louise, rent bikes at **Wilson Mountain Sports** (Samson Mall; ☎ 403/522-3636). In Jasper, the folks at **Vicious Cycle** (630 Connaught Dr.; ☎ 780/852-1111; www.viciouscanada.com) are the local experts on two-wheeling. They rent front-suspension mountain bikes that can also be used on roads. You can rent both road and mountain bikes from **Jasper Source for Sports** (406 Patricia St.; ☎ 780/852-3654).

BUSINESS HOURS Hours vary by shop, but as a general rule most open daily around 10am and stay open until at least 6pm. Shops in the Town of Banff usually stay open later. Most are open daily, though some close on Sunday.

CONSULATES & EMBASSIES The **U.S. Consulate** is at Ste. 1000, 615 Macleod Trail SW, Calgary (☎ 403/266-8962). The **British Consulate** is at Ste. 3000, 150 6th Ave. SW, Calgary (☎ 403/705-1755). The **Irish Consulate** is at 3803 8th A St. SW, Calgary (☎ 403/243-2970). The nearest **Australian Consulate** is at 2050-1075 W. Georgia St., Vancouver (☎ 604/694-6160). The consulate of **New Zealand** is at 1050 W. Pender St., Vancouver (☎ 604/684-7388).

CURRENCY EXCHANGE Currency exchange counters can be found at the airport, but you'll get a better rate just using ATMs or at the **Custom House Global Foreign Exchange,** at 211 Banff Ave. (☎ 403/760-6630).

In Jasper, there is a currency exchange house in **Whistlers Inn** (105 Miette Ave.; ☎ 780/852-3361). Be sure to check current exchange rates before your trip via www.xe.com or any of the other major currency trackers.

CUSTOMS Non-Canadian residents will pass through **Canada Border Services** (☎ 800/461-9999 or 204/983-3500; www.cbsa-asfc.gc.ca) upon arriving in the country. If you're concerned about items you intend to bring into the country, check the website's "Information for Visitors" section. U.S. citizens will pass through **U.S. Customs** (☎ 877/CBP-5511 [227-5511]; www.cbp.gov) on departure from Canada. The standard personal duty-free allowance for U.S. citizens returning from Canada is US$800. There are also limits on the amount of alcoholic beverages (usually 1L), cigarettes (1 carton), cigars (100 total, and no Cubans), and other tobacco products you may include in your personal duty-free exemption. **Joint Customs declarations** are possible for family members traveling together. For instance, for a husband and wife with two children, the total duty-free exemption would be US$3,200. Note that most meat or meat products, fruits, plants, vegetables, or plant-derived products will be seized by U.S. Customs agents unless they're accompanied by an import license from a U.S. government agency.

For more specifics, visit the **U.S. Customs Service** website (www. cbp.gov). U.K. citizens should visit the **U.K. Customs and Excise** site (www.hmce.gov.uk), Australians should go to the **Australia Customs Service** (www.customs.gov. au), Kiwis should check the **New Zealand Customs Service** (www. customs.govt.nz), and citizens of Ireland should check the **Irish Revenue** site (www.revenue.ie).

DENTISTS Most major hotels have a dentist on call. **Banff Dental Care** is at 220 Bear St. (☎ 403/762-3979). Call first for an appointment. The clinic is open Monday and Wednesday 8am to 5pm, Tuesday and Thursday 9am to 6pm, and Friday 8am to 1pm.

DINING Eating out will be one of your highlights in Banff. For the most popular spots, reservations are recommended, and are essential on Saturday evenings or long weekends.

DOCTORS Hotels usually have a doctor on call. **Alpine Medical Clinic,** 201A-211 Bear St. (☎ 403/762-3155), is a drop-in clinic open Monday through Thursday 8:30am to 7pm, Friday 8am to 5pm, and weekends 9am to 5pm.

ELECTRICITY Outlets and voltage (110 volts AC) are the same in Canada as in the United States, so laptops, chargers, hair dryers, and other small appliances from the U.S. will work just fine. Appliances from some other countries that work on a different voltage will require an adapter and/or converter.

EMBASSIES See "Consulates & Embassies" above.

EMERGENCIES For emergencies in Canada dial ☎ **911.**

EVENT LISTINGS Event listings are posted online by the **Banff–Lake Louise Tourism Bureau** at www. banfflakelouise.com. The free local weekly newspaper **Rocky Mountain Outlook** (www.rmoutlook.com) also is a great source for updated arts, sports, and community events. It's published on Thursdays and available throughout Banff.

FAMILY TRAVEL Banff and the Canadian Rockies are fantastically kid-friendly. Family travel websites include **Family Travel Forum** (www. familytravelforum.com), a comprehensive site that offers customized trip planning; **Family Travel Network** (www.familytravelnetwork. com), an online magazine providing travel tips; and **Travelwithyourkids. com** (www.travelwithyourkids.com), a comprehensive site written by

---

parents for parents offering sound advice for long-distance and international travel with children.

GAY & LESBIAN TRAVELERS **Banff Pride** (☎ 800/958-9621) is a social networking group (www.facebook.com/BanffPRIDE) for Banff residents and visitors. **Banff Gay Weddings** (☎ 403/609-3896; www.banffgayweddings.com) organizes same-sex ceremonies and events. Banff and its neighboring towns are gay-friendly.

HOLIDAYS Alberta has 12 public holidays throughout the year, when banks, government offices, schools, and some shops are closed: New Year's Day (Jan 1), Family Day (third Mon in Feb), Good Friday (the Fri before Easter), Easter Monday (the day after), Victoria Day (the Mon before May 25), Canada Day (July 1), Heritage Day (first Mon in Aug), Labour Day (first Mon in Sept), Thanksgiving (second Mon in Oct), Remembrance Day (Nov 11), Christmas (Dec 25), and Boxing Day (Dec 26).

INSURANCE The cost of travel insurance varies widely, depending on the destination, the cost and length of your trip, your age and health, and the type of trip you're taking. You can get estimates from various providers through **Insure-MyTrip.com** (www.insuremytrip.com). Enter your trip cost and dates, your age, and other information, for prices from more than a dozen companies.

Medical Insurance: Most U.S. health plans do not provide coverage outside of the U.S., and the ones that do often require you to pay for services upfront and reimburse you only after you return home. As a safety net, you may want to buy travel medical insurance from providers like **MEDEX Assistance** (☎ 410/453-6300; www.medexassist.com) or **Travel Assistance International** (☎ 800/821-2828; www.travelassistance.com).

Trip-Cancellation Insurance: Trip-cancellation insurance typically covers you if you have to back out of a trip (due to illness, for example), if your travel supplier goes bankrupt, if there's a natural disaster, or if your government advises against travel to your destination. Some plans cover cancellations for any reason. **TravelSafe** (☎ 888/885-7233; www.travelsafe.com) offers both types of coverage. **Expedia** (www.expedia.com) also offers any-reason cancellation coverage for its air-hotel packages. Other recommended insurers include: **Access America** (☎ 866/807-3982; www.accessamerica.com); **Travel Guard International** (☎ 800/826-4919; www.travelguard.com); **Travel Insured International** (☎ 800/243-3174; www.travelinsured.com); and **Travelex Insurance Services** (☎ 888/457-4602; www.travelex-insurance.com).

Lost-Luggage Insurance: If your luggage is lost, immediately file a lost-luggage claim at the airport, detailing the luggage contents. Most airlines require that you report delayed, damaged, or lost baggage within 4 hours of arrival. On international flights, baggage coverage is limited to approximately US$9.07 per pound, up to approximately US$635 per checked bag. If you plan to check items more valuable than what's covered by the standard liability, see if your homeowner's policy covers your valuables, or get baggage insurance as part of your comprehensive travel-insurance package.

INTERNET ACCESS Almost all hotels, cafes, and restaurants in the Canadian Rockies now provide free Wi-Fi. There's even free Wi-Fi in some Parks Canada campgrounds.

The Savvy Traveler

LIQUOR LAWS The legal drinking age in Alberta is 18. In British Columbia it is 19. Bars, lounges, and restaurants that serve alcohol all close between midnight and 2am, depending on when they got their liquor license. Hard liquor, beer and wine are available at privately owned liquor stores in Alberta. Specialty wine stores (p 86 lists some of the best) mostly stick to the grape, but usually also carry a small selection of beer and spirits.

LOST PROPERTY Lost items are often turned in to the **Town of Banff**, where they are kept for 30 days. Contact ☎ 403/762-1218 daily between 8am and 6pm for inquiries. There is also an online Lost Property Report available at the town's website, www.banff.ca. Outside the Town of Banff, try **Parks Canada** at ☎ 403/762-1550.

If you lose your passport, contact your country's embassy or consulate immediately (see "Consulates & Embassies," p 167).

MAIL & POSTAGE Mailing a letter within Canada costs 85¢. To the U.S., it's $1.20. To all other international destinations, it's $2.50. The main **post office** in Banff is at 204 Buffalo St. (☎ 403/762-2586; www.canadapost.ca), across from Central Park. You can also buy stamps at many drugstores and convenience stores.

MONEY Canada's money is denominated the same as U.S. dollars, except its C$1 and C$2 denominations are coins rather than bills. The C$1 coin is known as a "loonie" as it has the image of a common loon on one side. The C$2 coin is known as a "toonie," for obvious comedic reasons. For exchange rates, see "Currency Exchange," p 167.

NEWSPAPERS & MAGAZINES The major newspapers in Alberta are the **Calgary Herald** (www. calgaryherald.com) and the **Edmonton Journal** (www.theprovince. com), which both publish 7 days a week.

The local weekly newspapers in Banff are **the Rocky Mountain Outlook** (www.rmoutlook.com), which publishes every Thursday, and **the Banff Crag and Canyon** (www.thecragandcanyon.com), which hits stands on Tuesdays.

PARKING See "Getting Around: By Car," p 166.

PASSPORTS U.S. citizens traveling to Canada by any means— air, sea, car, bus, train, or on foot— will need a passport but no visa. The same applies for citizens of the United Kingdom, Australia, Ireland, and New Zealand. If you're a citizen of another country, check the **Canada Border Services Agency** website, www.cbsa-asfc.gc.ca/travel-voyage, for specific requirements.

For safety, make two photocopies of your passport before leaving home. Take one set with you as a backup (keeping it separate from the original) and leave one at home.

PERMITS Every visitor to a national park is required to have a permit (also known as a pass). You can pick one up at a park gate or information center inside the park. Permits are valid in all Canadian Rocky Mountain national parks (Banff, Jasper, Yoho, Kootenay, Waterton Lakes, and Glacier national parks). A day pass costs $9.80 for adults, $8.30 for seniors, and $4.90 for children. More economical is the Annual Pass, which is a good idea if you're planning to stay for a few days and visit more than one park. It's valid for 1 year from the purchase date for unlimited entries to every one of Canada's national parks, coast to coast. Individual rates are $68 for adults, $58 for seniors, and $33 for children ages 6 to 12. The pass is free for children ages 5 and under. For groups of 2 to 7, this pass costs $136, making it the best deal for most visitors.

Permits are also required for backcountry camping and fishing inside the National Parks. For more information, visit www.pc.gc.ca.

PET-FRIENDLY TRAVEL While there are a few hotels in Banff that welcome pets, in general the Canadian Rockies aren't particularly pet-friendly. This is mainly due to the importance placed on the health of the local wildlife populations. Keep your dog on a leash at all times, especially in campgrounds and on hiking trails. To wildlife like elk, wolves, bears, and cougars, your dog may look an awful lot like dinner. Avoid any areas in the parks where the potential for wildlife encounters is high (ask at an information center), and take your dog for a walk only during daylight hours. Do not leave your dog unattended outside. Unrestrained pets have been known to harass wildlife, provoke attacks, and endanger people. And please pick up after your pooch—the "leave no trace" principle applies to pets, too.

PHARMACIES The biggest pharmacy in the Town of Banff is **Rexall Drug Store,** lower level of Cascade Plaza (317 Banff Ave.; ☎ 403/762-2245).

POLICE Call ☎ **911** for emergencies.

SAFETY Don't drink the water from any streams, rivers, or lakes in Banff or Jasper national parks. A waterborne parasite called *Giardia lamblia* can cause an illness known in Canada as "beaver fever." It is transmitted via infected animal feces and can cause serious and prolonged gastrointestinal problems.

Also be on the lookout for **wood ticks**—small, flat-bodied, spider-like insects that bite humans and can carry **Rocky Mountain spotted fever** and **Lyme disease** (although the latter is rare in the northern Rockies). They usually abound in dry, grassy slopes in the spring. If you're hiking through such an area, give yourself a good once-over at the end of the day. If in doubt, drop by the **Mineral Springs Hospital** in Banff to see a doctor (301 Lynx St.; ☎ 403/762-2222). In Jasper, go to **Seton General Hospital** (518 Robson St.; ☎ 780/852-3344). There has been no evidence of West Nile virus in the Canadian Rockies.

Hiking in the mountains is so beautiful that it may make you feel lightheaded. But lightheadedness may also be a sign of **altitude sickness.** Although elevations in the Canadian Rockies aren't as high as in the Colorado and Montana Rockies, you can still feel the altitude. People with severe heart or lung conditions should take note. Others should bring along some headache medicine and drink plenty of water.

You'll also be closer to the sun in the mountains, so wear a **sun hat** and **sunscreen.** Beyond the sun, cold and rain are the other weather factors that could hamper your holiday. Check the latest weather forecast before heading out. Always pack a rain jacket and warm clothing in your daypack. And always carry a **first-aid kit,** both in your car and in your pack. At the very least, it should include latex gloves (to prevent spreading infections), butterfly bandages, sterile gauze pads, adhesive tape, antibiotic ointment, pain relievers (for kids and adults), alcohol pads, knife, scissors, and tweezers.

Hiking in Banff involves moving through bear country and you should be prepared to encounter a bear at any time. Carry bear spray and know how to use it. Make noise while you hike, keep your dog on a leash and hike in groups. Pick up the "Hiking in Bear Country" pamphlet from Parks Canada for more information.

In terms of personal safety in the mountains, be aware that almost any slope is a potential **avalanche** chute—and even small avalanches can be deadly. Drivers should avoid stopping in places where there are signs that read NO STOPPING, AVALANCHE AREA, and anyone venturing into the backcountry—especially in winter—should know how to recognize and travel in avalanche terrain. Call ☎ 403/762-1460 in Banff or ☎ 780/852-6176 in Jasper for the latest avalanche hazard reports from Parks Canada.

There is also a risk of getting hit by falling rock and ice or slipping into a glacier crevasse, particularly in Jasper National Park. Do not ignore the signs telling you to stay back from the **Angel Glacier** at **Mt. Edith Cavell** or the **Athabasca Glacier,** both in Jasper. These can be—and have been—deadly.

Don't leave valuables in your car or unattended in public places. This also applies to hiking trail heads. The Canadian Government website (**www.safecanada.ca**) has a list of safety tips in case you need something to worry about.

SENIOR TRAVELERS Shops, hotels, attractions, and services throughout Western Canada often offer discounts for people 65 and over.

SMOKING Smoking is prohibited in all public places in Alberta and British Columbia, including bars, clubs, and restaurants.

TAXES All hotels, restaurants, gift shops, and services charge the 5% goods and services tax (GST) on all purchases. (**Note:** A program that allowed foreigners to receive a rebate for the GST spent during their time in Canada was cancelled in 2007.) There is no provincial sales tax in Alberta. In British Columbia, an additional provincial sales tax of 7% is charged on purchased goods.

TELEPHONES **Dialing within Alberta** requires you to use full 10-digit phone numbers, including the area code, of which there are two in Alberta: 403 and 780. To reach the British Columbia side of the Canadian Rockies, first dial 250. **Phoning between the U.S. and Canada** requires no special trick: Just dial 1 plus the area code and local number, as you would between states in the U.S. **To dial other countries** direct from Banff, dial the international access code (011), followed by the relevant country code (61 for Australia, 353 for Ireland, 64 for New Zealand, and 44 for the U.K.) and the local number with area code, if applicable. **To call Banff from outside North America,** dial the international access code (00 from the U.K., Ireland, or New Zealand, or 0011 from Australia), the country code (1), and then the local number with area code. For information on cellphone service, see "Cell Phones," p 164.

TIME ZONE Alberta and the B.C. Rockies are located in the Mountain time zone, 7 hours behind Greenwich Mean Time (changing to the Pacific time zone between Golden and Revelstoke). The area observes daylight saving time from the second Sunday in March to the first Sunday in November.

TIPPING Customary tipping amounts are the same in Banff and the rest of Canada as in major U.S. cities, with a target of 15% for restaurants and taxis. (Though many people round that up to 20%.) If porters help with your bags at hotels or airports, the usual tip is $1 per bag (or $2 if it's heavy).

TOILETS Public toilets are increasingly easy to find in Banff. In fact, there are now nine facilities dotted around the main area of town, including the Whyte Museum, the Public Library, and Central Park. You can also find facilities at the corner of Wolf Street and Banff Avenue, and in the Parks Canada Administration Building, just across the Bow River Bridge. In Lake Louise, there are facilities in the Visitor Centre, in the main parking lot at the lakeshore, and in the Fairmont Chateau Lake Louise.

TOURIST OFFICES The following on-the-ground tourist centers can help with information, maps, suggestions, and booking accommodations: **Banff Information Centre** is at 224 Banff Ave. (☎ 403/762-1550), and there is a similar location at the **Lake Louise Visitor Centre,** in Samson Mall, 101 Lake Louise Dr. (☎ 403/522-3833). **Jasper National Park's Information Centre** is at 500 Connaught Dr. (☎ 780/852-6716). Just before you enter Banff National Park, you can visit the **Travel Alberta Visitor Information Centre** in Canmore at 2801 Bow Valley Parkway (☎ 800/252-3782 or 403/678-5277), which is right off the Trans-Canada Hwy. 1.

TOURS Brewster (P.O. Box 1140, Banff, AB T1L 1J3; ☎ 877/791-5500 or 403/762-6700; www.brewster.ca) knows Banff better than any other tour operator and has a long history of guiding here to prove it. It offers many sightseeing tours in both Banff and Jasper. Taking even the 3-hour **Discover Banff with Banff Gondola tour** will teach you more than you'll ever learn on your own.

Discover Banff Tours (215 Banff Ave., P.O. Box 1566, Banff, AB T1L 1B5; ☎ 877/565-9372 or 403/760-5007; www.bannftours.com) leads small groups on interpretive tours of all the highlights in Banff National Park, including the Town of Banff, Lake Louise, and Moraine Lake, as well as the Icefields Parkway. Morning and evening wildlife-viewing tours are really nice.

TRAVELERS WITH DISABILITIES The museums and visitor centers in Banff are all wheelchair-accessible. Most hotels now have at least one wheelchair-accessible room. The **Upper Hot Springs** in Banff National Park and the Radium Hot Springs in Kootenay National Park are friendly to those with mobility restraints.

If you are planning on car camping, head for **Tunnel Mountain, Johnston Canyon, Lake Louise,** or **Waterfowl Lakes campgrounds.** In Jasper National Park, try **Whistlers, Wapiti,** or **Wabasso.**

Signs clearly mark which trails in the parks are paved. In Banff, try the asphalt-covered **Sundance Trail.** There is an adjustable-height viewing scope at **Bow Summit.** The Lakeside Trail at **Lake Louise** is another wheelchair-accessible trail. Wheelchair-friendly trails in Jasper include the **Clifford E. Lee Trail** at Lake Edith/Annette and the **Maligne Lake Trail,** as well as points along **Maligne Canyon,** at **Pyramid Island,** and the interpretive loop at the **Pocahontas Coal Mine Trail.**

WEIGHTS & MEASURES Canada uses the metric system. Remember: 1km = 0.62 miles, 1 liter = 0.26 gallons, 1 kilogram = 2.2 pounds, and Celsius temperatures are based on 0 being the freezing point (in Fahrenheit measurement it's 32).

A Brief **History**

175 MILLION YEARS AGO The Rocky Mountains are formed as the Pacific tectonic plate moves under the North American plate.

11,000 B.C. Early archeological records date the presence of peoples like the Crees, Kootenays, and Plains Blackfoot to have lived, fished, and hunted in the vast Rocky Mountains.

1754 The first recorded visit of a European to the Rockies is made by Anthony Hendy.

1800 Legendary explorer and mapmaker David Thompson explores the Bow Valley.

1841 George Simpson, the Governor of the Hudson's Bay Company, is the first known European to visit the Town of Banff area.

1871 As part of a deal to unite British Columbia with the rest of Canada, the Canadian government forms the Canadian Pacific Railway (CPR) to construct a railway across the new nation.

1882 Tom Wilson, a CPR guide, becomes the first non-Native man to see Lake Louise, with the help of his Stoney partner.

1883 Three railway workers stumble upon a series of hot springs on the lower slopes of Sulphur Mountain.

1885 Canada's first national park is formed in Banff, preserving 26 sq. km (10 sq. miles) surrounding the hot springs. The reserve is increased to 670 sq. km (259 sq. miles) in 1887 and 7,125 sq. km (2,751 sq. miles) in 1917.

1886 Construction of the Canadian Pacific Railway is completed. Banff is named after the Scottish district "Banffshire," birthplace of two of the CPR's directors, Lord Strathcona and George Stephen.

1888 The CPR opens the elegant log-framed 250-room Banff Springs Hotel, the most expensive hotel in the world at the time.

1890 A log cabin is built on the shores of Lake Louise, soon to be replaced by a larger "chateau."

1917 The Federal Government passes the first National Parks Act in the world.

1921 A road is completed linking Banff and Lake Louise, ushering in the era of car-based tourism.

1928 A log cabin is built at the site of today's Sunshine Village as a stopover for horse trekkers.

1936 Temple Lodge is built across the Bow Valley from Lake Louise, the beginning of the Lake Louise ski resort's history.

1941 The first rope tows are installed at Sunshine Village ski resort.

1956 The Trans-Canada Hwy. 1 is completed through Banff and Yoho national parks.

1961 Paving of the Icefields Parkway is completed.

1985 Banff, Jasper, Yoho, and Kootenay national parks, along with four adjacent provincial parks, are declared a World Heritage Site by the United Nations Educational, Scientific and Cultural Organization (UNESCO).

1990 Thanks to a joint agreement between local citizens and the federal and provincial governments, Banff becomes a self-governing municipality within the Province of Alberta, the only incorporated municipality within a Canadian national park.

1998 The Delirium Dive area, a mecca for extreme skiers, is re-opened at Sunshine Village.

1999 Parks Canada begins requiring hikers to travel in tight groups of four in high grizzly bear territory, especially around Moraine Lake during peak summer hiking season.

2007 Banff's downtown core undergoes a redevelopment to replaced dated infrastructure, making it more pedestrian friendly.

Airline Websites

AIR CANADA
www.aircanada.ca
ALASKA AIRLINES
www.alaskaair.com
AMERICAN AIRLINES
www.aa.com
BRITISH AIRWAYS
www.britishairways.com

DELTA AIR LINES
www.delta.com
FRONTIER AIRLINES
www.flyfrontier.com
UNITED AIRLINES
www.united.com
WESTJET
www.westjet.com

Index

See also Accommodations and Restaurant indexes, below.

Restaurants

Photo **Credits**

p 1: © Claire Dibble; p 2, top: © Andrew Hempstead; p 2, bottom: Courtesy Via Ferrata; p 4: © Serge Desrosiers/Frommers.com Community; p 5: © Andrew Hempstead; p 6: © CCinCalif./Frommers.com Community; p 7, 9: © Andrew Hempstead; p 10, top: © Claire Dibble; p 10, bottom: © Andrew Hempstead; p 11: Courtesy Fairmont Hotels & Resorts; p 13, top and bottom: © Andrew Hempstead; p 14: Courtesy Fairmont Hotels & Resorts; p 15: With Kind Permission Travel Alberta/Copithorne & Blakely; p 16, top: karamysh/Shutterstock.com; p 16, bottom: kavram/Shutterstock.com; p 17: © elleonora/Frommers.com Community; p 19: © Andrew Hempstead; p 20, top: © Claire Dibble; p 20, bottom: © Brian Leroy/Frommers.com Community; p 21: © Linda Plummer/Frommers.com Community; p 23: © kmaltagliati/Frommers.com Community; p 24: © Claire Dibble; p 25, top: © Claire Dibble; p 25, bottom: © Andrew Hempstead; p 26, top and bottom: © Claire Dibble; p 28: © Claire Dibble; p 29: © Andrew Hempstead; p 30: Courtesy Fairmont Hotels & Resorts; p 31: © Sue G. PR/Frommers.com Community; p 33: © Tando/Frommers.com Community; p 34: © Andrew Hempstead; p 35: © Matthewas/Frommers.com Community; p 37, 38 (top and bottom): © Andrew Hempstead; p 39: Courtesy of Fairmont Hotels & Resorts; p 41: © Andrew Hempstead; p 42, top: © Andrew Hempstead; p 42, bottom: Courtesy of Fairmont Hotels & Resorts; p 43: © Photo by Richard Halman, Courtesy Sunshine Village; p 45, 46 (top and bottom): © Claire Dibble; p 47: ca2hill/Shutterstock.com; p 48: Courtesy of Fairmont Hotels & Resorts; p 49: karamysh/Shutterstock.com; p 51: © Claire Dibble; p 52, top and bottom: © Andrew Hempstead; p 53: © Claire Dibble; p 54, top: © Andrew Hempstead; p 54, bottom: With Kind Permission Canada House Gallery; p 55: © Photo Don Lee, courtesy of the Banff Centre; p 57, top and bottom: © Claire Dibble; p 59: © Claire Dibble; p 61: © Andrew Hempstead; p 62: With Kind Permission Fairmont Chateau Lake Louise; p 63, 65: © Claire Dibble; p 66, top: © Andrew Hempstead; p 66, bottom: © Claire Dibble; p 67: VDV/Shutterstock.com; p 69: Courtesy Maple Leaf Grill and Lounge; p 70: © Andrew Hempstead; p 71, top: Courtesy of Fairmont Hotels & Resorts; p 71, bottom: With Kind Permission The Bear Street Tavern; p 72, top: © Andrew Hempstead; p 72, bottom: Kelly MacDonald, Courtesy Juniper Bistro; p 73: © Photo by Heather McCoy, Courtesy Nourish; p 74: Courtesy Saltlik; p 75: Paul Zizka; p 77: © Photo by Paul Zizka, Courtesy Num-Ti-Jah Lodge; p 78: © Andrew Hempstead; p 79: Courtesy Fairmont Hotels & Resorts; p 80, top: With Kind Permission Fairmont Chateau Lake Louise; p 80, bottom: Courtesy Banff Lodging Co.; p 81, top: © Andrew Hempstead; p 81, bottom: Courtesy Post Hotel & Spa; p 82: Courtesy Rimrock Resort Hotels; p 83: P Zizka/Parks Canada; p 85: © Andrew Hempstead; p 86, 87, 88: © Claire Dibble; p 89: © Photo Donald Lee, Courtesy of The Banff Centre; p 90: Courtesy Aurora Nightclub; p 91: © Claire Dibble; p 93, top: © Andrew Hempstead; p 93, bottom: Courtesy Kananaskis Country Golf Course; p 94, 96 (top and bottom): © Claire Dibble; p 97: © Andrew Hempstead; p 99: © Claire Dibble; p 100, top: © Andrew Hempstead; p 100, bottom: © Claire Dibble; p 102, top: © Barbara Larmon Failing/Frommers.com Community; p 102, bottom: Courtesy Canadian Rockies Hot Springs; p 104 (top and bottom), 105: © Claire Dibble; p 107: kavram/Shutterstock.com; p 108: © Claire Dibble; p 109: Png Studio Photography/Shutterstock.com; p 111, top: © Claire Dibble; p 111, bottom: Courtesy Kootenay River Runners; p 113, top and bottom: © Andrew Hempstead; p 114, top: Courtesy Kootenay Park Lodge; p 114, bottom: © Claire Dibble; p 115: © Claire Dibble; p 117, top: © Claire Dibble; p 117, bottom: © Andrew Hempstead; p 118, top: © Claire Dibble; p 118, bottom: Courtesy River Café; p 119: Courtesy Calgary Stampede; p 121: © Claire Dibble; p 123, 124: © Andrew Hempstead; p 125, top: With Kind Permission Fairmont Palliser; p 125, bottom: Courtesy Kensington Riverside Inn; p 127, top and bottom: © Andrew Hempstead; p 128, 129, 130 (top and bottom): © Andrew Hempstead; p 131: Courtesy Fairmont Hotels & Resorts; p 132: © Andrew Hempstead; p 133: © Claire Dibble; p 135: Courtesy Horsethief Creek Pub; p 136, top: Courtesy Kicking Horse Lodge; p 136, bottom: Courtesy Cathedral Mountain Lodge; p 137: Courtesy Copper Horse Lodge; p 138, top: Courtesy of Canadian Rocky Mountain Resorts; p 138, bottom: Courtesy Lake O'Hara Lodge; p 139, 142: © Claire Dibble; p 144, top: © Gerry M. Bates/Frommers.com Community; p 144, bottom: © Andrew Hempstead; p 146, top: © Claire Dibble; p 146, bottom: © Andrew Hempstead; p 147, 148 (top and bottom), 149, 151, 152: © Claire Dibble; p 153, top: Courtesy Via Ferrata; p 153, bottom: Courtesy Fairmont Hotels & Resorts; p 154: © Claire Dibble; p 155, top: © Andrew Hempstead; p 155, bottom: © Claire Dibble; p 157: Courtesy Banff Norquay; p 158: © Photo by Sean Hannah, Courtesy Sunshine Village; p 159: Courtesy Fairmont Hotels & Resorts; p 160, top: Al Parker | Dreamstime.com; p 160, bottom: Courtesy Fairmont Hotels & Resorts; p 161: © Andrew Hempstead